Contents

Introduction

Young children learn by doing. Pre-school and primary age children respond to color, action, and involvement. Manipulation of objects and touchable stimuli reinforce and personalize the spoken word. With this in mind *Children Discover the Mass* helps children to learn the parts of the Mass, as well as appreciate its order, beauty, mystery, and community through craft activities that accompany instruction and discussion.

Children Discover the Mass is organized into five chapters, highlighting the main parts of the Mass in chapters two through five. Chapter 1 "Before We Begin Mass," is a preface to the liturgy. It is important to begin with the three lessons in this chapter as they provide not only the main craft objects (e.g., church, altar, vestments) needed for Mass, but lessons previewing the order of the Mass to allow children to view its parts. Children learn that many different kinds of people come together in unity at Mass. The craft pieces completed with this chapter are freestanding and moveable, enabling the children to manipulate and role play with the figures. These pieces form the core of the liturgical ensemble the children will make in the remainder of the lessons.

Chapters 2 through 5 present lessons and crafts of the Mass in sequential order. All lessons begin with preliminary background instruction reinforcing *why* this element of the Mass is important and *why* we interact in a specific way. Secondly, suggestions are given on what can be said to the children to foster understanding and discussion. Directions for the craft activity are also included. Next, a meaningful craft, with concise directions, affords children firsthand experience. Finally, review questions provide for follow-up and promote additional consideration.

On the craft pages themselves, the directions are repeated. Often secondary or extension ideas are included on the reverse side of the craft page.

This systematic and enjoyable approach will help children better comprehend the wonderful celebration of the Mass. In an atmosphere of fun and creativity, young children will come to know the Mass. The activities found in this book promote a sense of purpose and understanding for *what* we say and do during celebration and for *why* we celebrate.

Children Discover the Mass may be used to supplement any curriculum already in place. Lessons and activities may be completed in a large or small group catechetical setting that is either formal or informal. Too, parents may wish to employ this book for personal home use to introduce the Mass or to reinforce and enhance activities already developed in the classroom setting.

How to Use the Book

As mentioned, *Children Discover the Mass* can be used in many ways. It is a resource intended for children from pre-school to primary ages. Listed below are ten suggestions for using this book:

- Duplicate craft pages on slightly heavier than average paper. The person figures may be duplicated on card stock.
- Set the copy machine for double sided reproduction, as each craft has information on its reverse side. Duplicate on both sides.
- In general, the dark lines on the craft pages should be **cut**. The dotted lines on the craft pages should be **folded**.
- Complete the lessons and crafts in sequence to show the order of the liturgy.
- Make and keep a complete set of activities on hand to use as a model for the children and to help you teach each lesson. (You may wish to remove stands and place felt on the back of the craft figures to allow for felt board storytelling.)
- Share the content of the lesson in your own words based on the "Say to the Students" presentations.
- Check the students' retention of the lesson by asking them the Review Questions included with each lesson *after* they have completed the craft. Extend the lessons using the special notes on the back of the crafts.

- Collect each child's completed crafts into a notebook or folder. When they have completed all of the lessons and crafts, they will have their own Mass set collection.
- Record the dates you complete each lesson and any evaluation notes you have on the lesson and craft.
- Remind the children to look and listen closely for the part of Mass they have learned about when they next attend Mass. Some of the craft pages lend themselves to being taken by the children with them to Mass. The "My Mass Book" (see below) also works well for that purpose.

My Mass Book

A separate "My Mass Book" for the children is included in the Appendix. Duplicate all the consecutive pages back to back. Then have the children fold the pages to form a book. Add two staples on the center fold.

The children can color several of the figures in "My Mass Book." There are some other pages on which the children can write Mass responses. Have the children color each page from "My Mass Book" as they coincide with the related lesson. Encourage them to take these books with them to Mass.

Lessons, Crafts, Cutouts, and More!

Children Discover the Mass

Mary Doerfler Dall

ave maria press   Notre Dame, Indiana

Dedication
For Dan,
a constant source of strength and support.

Acknowledgments

Thanks to my parents, Henry and Mary, who always served as living, loving examples of Christian principles.
Thanks to the many CCD and Sunday School teachers along the way who have been a source of loving inspiration.
Thanks to Sue Pratt, Director of Religious Education at St. Stephen Catholic Church, Winter Springs, Florida.
Thanks to my editor, Michael Amodei, for his valuable help and insight that expanded and strengthened this project.

International Standard Book Number: 0-87793-948-9

Text and cover design by Brian C. Conley

Printed and bound in the United States of America.

Library of Congress Cataloging-in-Publication Data

Dall, Mary Doerfler.
        Children discover the Mass : lessons, crafts, cutouts, and more! /
Mary Doerfler Dall.
        p. cm.
        ISBN 0-87793-948-9
        1. Mass--Celebration--Study and teaching (Elementary)--Activity
programs. 2. Christian education of children. I. Title.
BX2238.5 .D35   2000
268'.432--dc21

                                                                          00-008681
                                                                               CIP

1

Before We Begin Mass

Lesson 1: The Church Is God's House

Lesson 2: Mass Mobile

Lesson 3: Preparing for Mass

Lesson 1:
The Church Is God's House

Background

The building that we call "church" comes in a variety of designs and structures. The purpose of having a special building for worship is that it provides us with a space large enough for us to physically come together. The structure of the church provides a sanctuary for an altar, places for the community to sit, room for a choir, and separate areas for personal prayer and devotion.

Say to the Students:

Mass can be celebrated anywhere. It has been said in private homes, on battlefields, in gymnasiums and on the top of mountains. Usually Mass is celebrated in a special building that we call a church. This is the best setting for the Mass since a church can hold many people comfortably.

Churches come in all shapes and sizes. Some are modern, some are old; many have stained glass windows while others may have no windows at all. No matter what size, shape, or design, all churches are special since a church is a place where we come together to worship the Lord and it is the place where Jesus lives and the Blessed Sacrament is kept. The church is truly God's house!

Craft Directions for The Church Is God's House (pages 13-16)

1. Color the church. Cut out the church on bold lines.
2. Trace the letters, color, and cut out the heart.
3. Glue the edges only of the church and steeple to page 15, "The Church Is God's House." Do not glue the doors.
4. Open the doors and fold them back.
5. Glue the heart in place behind doors.

Optional: Provide a large piece of poster paper for each child. Have the children glue their finished projects on the poster paper and decorate the rest of the paper with drawings of facilities (e.g., school, parish center, rectory) on parish grounds.

Review Questions

- Why don't all churches look the same?
- What is a favorite part of your church?
- How do you feel loved when you are at your church?

Lesson 2:
Mass Mobile

Background

The Mass is divided into two main parts, the Liturgy of the Word and the Liturgy of the Eucharist. Prior to these parts, we greet one another and begin our worship in the name of the Father, and of the Son, and of the Holy Spirit. A "Mass Mobile" serves as a visual representation of the main parts of the Mass and the greeting.

Say to the Students:

You have many special events in your life. When you go to a birthday party, someone greets you at the door and invites you inside. While you are at the party, there is a special time for singing the birthday song and blowing out candles. Another time is set aside for opening gifts. There may be a time for playing games.

In the same way, the Mass is also made up of special parts. When we first arrive at Mass, we say hello to one another. We say special prayers and sing the songs chosen for that day. The first part of the Mass is the Liturgy of the Word. Liturgy is a word that means "work of the people" because everyone at Mass has a special job. We listen to readings from the Old and New Testaments of the Bible. A second main part of the Mass is set aside for us to remember the sacrifice Jesus made for us and to rejoice in the new life Jesus gained for us by dying, rising, and ascending to heaven. The Liturgy of the Eucharist uses the words Jesus said at the Last Supper. Jesus is present in the form of bread and wine. We join in communion with God and one another.

Craft Directions for Mass Mobile (pages 17-18)

1. Lightly color the three pieces.
2. Cut out the three pieces on the bold lines.
3. Hole punch each piece on the X's.
4. Place the "Hello" at the top, the book in the middle, and the chalice at the bottom of the mobile.
5. String the three pieces together with yarn.

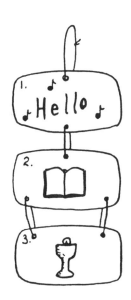

Review Questions

• How do you greet others when you come to Mass?
• What are the two main parts of the Mass?
• What special meal celebration that Jesus had with his disciples is remembered in the Liturgy of the Eucharist?

Lesson 3:
Preparing for Mass

Background

Over the year the Church reveals in its liturgy the mystery of our redemption. The Church Year is marked by seasons: Advent, Christmas, Lent, Easter (including the Triduum), and Ordinary Time. Each season has particular colors for vestments and altar linens: violet for Advent and Lent, white for Christmas and Easter, and green for Ordinary Time.

Mass is celebrated every day of the Church Year except for Good Friday. Sunday, also called "The Lord's Day," celebrates the first day of the week and takes its origin from the day Christ rose from the dead. Readings for the Liturgy of the Word follow the liturgical church calendar year. The readings are divided into three cycles, so that over a three-year period, the Church will hear a good portion of the Bible read at Mass.

Say to the Students:

Every Mass includes the Liturgy of the Word and the Liturgy of the Eucharist. The Bible readings change with the days and seasons. The vestments—the clothing worn by the priest—also change in color between the seasons of Advent (violet), Christmas (white), Lent (violet), Easter (white), and Ordinary Time (green).

One of the beauties of the Mass is that in this celebration of God's love for us, we combine many voices and talents to make each liturgy special. We use certain items during Mass to remind us of the holiness of the celebration. Many people, working together, make the Mass special. We come together with many helpers to celebrate God's love.

(Read or summarize each section to the children to explain the items used at Mass that are also a part of the craft display that follows.)

The Altar The altar is a big table, much like a family's dining table. It is in the middle of the sanctuary ("holy place") so everyone can see what is going on. One or two candles remind us that Jesus is the light of the world. Most importantly, the altar holds the bread and wine for the consecration. *(see page 19)*

Things on the Altar The cup the priest uses for the wine is called the *chalice*. The plate the priest uses for the blessed bread is called the *paten*. Small pitchers, called *cruets*, are used to pour water and wine. The priest reads from the Mass book called the *Sacramentary*. It is on the altar too. *(see page 19)*

The Priest The priest is our celebrant. That means he is the one who will lead us to celebrate the Mass as one people. He wears certain clothes called vestments. *(see page 21)*

Vestments Vestments are the priest's special clothes. The colors of the vestments tell us which season of the Church Year it is. *(see page 21)*

Altar servers Altar servers are boys and girls who want to show their love for God in a special way by helping at Mass. These altar servers learn the parts of the Mass so that they can help the priest at the altar. They light candles, carry the cross, hold the book, and do anything else they are asked to do during the Mass. *(see page 23)*

Choir The group of singers is the choir. This group of people can also include the choir director, musicians, and a cantor. *(see page 27)*

Cantor This is a person who sings solo (alone) and leads special parts of the Mass. *(see page 27)*

Musicians These are the people who play musical instruments, including the piano, organ, violins, and other instruments. Each Mass can be different. Some Masses may have no music. *(see page 27)*

Choir Director This is the person who helps keep all of the music, the singers, the cantor, and everyone singing together. *(see page 27)*

Eucharistic Ministers Eucharistic ministers help the priest give out the blessed bread and wine of communion. They take a class to learn how to handle holy things properly and then they are given this name because of the special job they have. Eucharistic ministers may also bring communion to sick members of the community who are unable to come to Mass. *(see page 25)*

Lector The person who brings the Lectionary (book of readings) to the front in the opening possession and who reads the first and second reading is called the *lector*. *(see page 25)*

Greeters/Ushers The greeters say hello and make us feel welcome in the church. The ushers guide us to our seats. They help collect our offerings. In many churches, ushers and greeters distribute the church bulletin so that everyone can be reminded of upcoming events at the parish. *(see page 25)*

Lectionary There are certain Bible readings for each Mass. They are contained in the *Lectionary*, the book of readings. You can go to any place in the world and know that the Mass will be celebrated in the same general way with the same Bible readings. It may be in a different language but if you know the Bible story for the day, you will understand.

Note: Encourage the children to identify helpers they may recognize from Mass. For example, perhaps their religion teacher is also a cantor or their parent is a lector.

Craft Directions for Preparing for Mass (pages 19-28)

1. Color and cut out the altar and items (page 19). Cut the slits on the altar (A-E). Insert the pieces into the proper slits and fold.
2. Color and cut out the priest and vestments *(see page 21)*. Fold the vestments on the dotted lines and slip them over the priest's head. Fold the stole on the dotted line. Slip it over the priest's head and the vestments.
3. Color and cut out the altar servers and vestments (page 21). Fold the chasubles on the dotted lines and slip them over the heads of the altar servers. Cut out the stands, fold on the dotted lines, and glue to the back of the altar servers.
4. Color and cut out the other helpers (pages 25-28). Fold stands on dotted lines.

Review Questions

- What is the sanctuary?
- Why is the altar in the very center of the sanctuary?
- What helper would you like to be at Mass someday?

The Church
(God's House)

Directions:
1. Color the church. Cut out the church on bold lines.
2. Trace the letters, color, and cut out the heart.
3. Glue the edges only of the church and steeple to page 15, "The Church Is God's House." Do not glue the doors.
4. Open the doors and fold them back.
5. Glue the heart in place behind the doors.

The Church Is God's House

We can pray anywhere and at any time. But, when we come to church we set aside a special place and time to make holy. We say, "I will come to God's house. I will come to church to be closer to Jesus, who is present there. I will worship and praise God with others who believe."

Glue church here

Draw a picture of your own parish church.

Mass Mobile

Introduction
Hello

The Liturgy of the Word
The Book

The Liturgy of the Eucharist
Host and Chalice

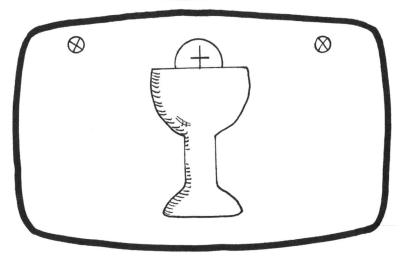

Directions:
1. Lightly color the three pieces.
2. Cut out the three pieces on the bold lines.
3. Hole punch each piece on the X's.
4. Place the "Hello" at the top, the book in the middle, and the chalice at the bottom of the mobile.
5. String the three pieces together with yarn.

1   *Introduction*

2   *Liturgy of the Word*

3   *The Liturgy of the Eucharist*

Next to the "1" draw some music notes, next to the "2" draw a book, and next to the "3" draw a host and chalice.

The Altar

E

C

c

A

B

E

B

D

+

D

Things on the Altar

Directions:

1. Color and cut out the altar and items
2. Cut the slits on the altar (A-E).
3. Insert the pieces into the proper slits and fold
   (A=candle; B=candle;
   C=chalice; D=flowers; E=cruets).

The altar is a table much like a family dining table. It is in the center of the sanctuary (holy place) so everyone can see what is going on. Candles on or near the altar remind us that Jesus is the light of the world. Most importantly, the altar holds the bread and wine for the consecration. The cup the priest uses is the *chalice*. The plate the priest uses is the *paten*. The paten holds the host. Small pitchers, called *cruets*, are used to pour water and wine. The priest reads from the Mass book, called the *Sacramentary*. It is on the altar too.

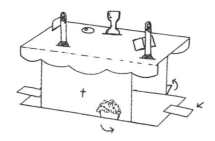

Priest

Vestments

chasubles

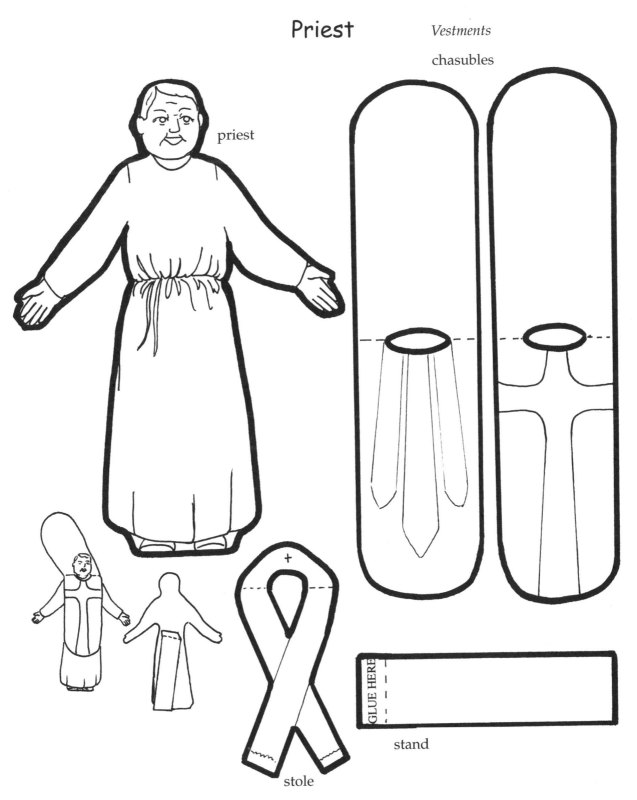

priest

stole

stand

Directions:
1. Color and cut out the priest and vestments.
2. Fold the vestments (chasuble) on the dotted lines and slip them over the priest's head.
3. Fold the stole on the dotted line. Slip it over the priest's head and the vestments.

Our Celebrant

The Priest

Chasuble   Chasuble

stole

Make and decorate your own vestments. Use the vestments you have cut out for a pattern.
Using this priest pattern, make a priest doll that resembles your own parish priest.

Altar Servers

Altar Server

Altar Server

GLUE HERE

GLUE HERE

stand

stand

vestment

vestment

Directions:
1. Color and cut out the altar servers and vestments.
2. Fold the chasubles on the dotted lines and slip them over the heads of the altar servers.
3. Cut out the stands, fold on the dotted lines, and glue to the back of the altar servers.

altar server   altar server

chasuble   chasuble

- Find a photo of you that is about the same size as these altar servers. Cut out the photo and put the vestments on your photo. Or, cut out a photo of your face to put on the altar server.
- Trace around one of the altar servers and draw your own face and hairstyle on it.

Other Helpers

Directions:
1. Color and cut out the other helpers.
2. Fold stands on dotted lines.

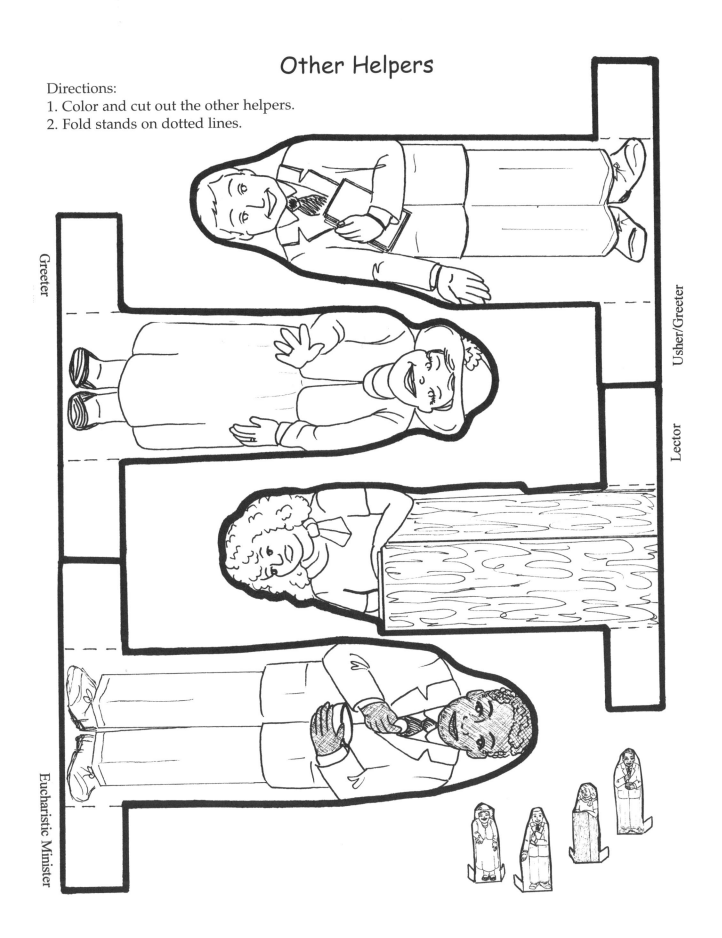

Greeter

Usher/Greeter

Lector

Eucharistic Minister

Eucharistic Minister, Lector, Usher, Greeter

The usher helps us find a place to sit and distributes church bulletins.

The greeter welcomes us to the church.

The lector reads the first and second readings at Mass.

The eucharistic minister helps to distribute communion.

Other Helpers

Choir Director, Choir, and Musicians

Cantor

Directions:
1. Color and cut out the other helpers.
2. Fold stands on dotted lines.

Choir and Musicians

The cantor sings alone during special parts of the Mass.

The choir director, choir, and musicians work together to make
the music a beautiful part of each liturgy.
The choir director leads the cantor, choir, and musicians.

The musicians accompany the sung music and often play music
without singing to help us think and pray.

2

Introductory Rites

Lesson 4: Opening Procession

Lesson 5: Greeting

Lesson 6: Penitential Rite

Lesson 7: Lord, Have Mercy

Lesson 8: Glory to God

Lesson 4:
Opening Procession

Background

The Mass begins with everyone standing. The priest, standing in the rear of the church, leads the people in the Sign of the Cross. Then he and the other liturgical ministers process to the sanctuary as an opening song is sung. They all bow in front of the altar. The priest and the other liturgical ministers process to the altar. They all bow. The priest kisses the altar as a sign of love and respect for Jesus. The lector places the Lectionary at the lectern, the place for readings.

Say to the Students:

We all stand, pray the Sign of the Cross, and sing a song to begin Mass. The music says hello. It says welcome. Often there is a choir and the music is chosen just for that day. The priest, the lector, and the altar servers walk in a procession to the sanctuary. The lector holds the Lectionary, a book containing the Bible readings to be read during the Liturgy of the Word.

Most of the time we stand and watch as the procession comes up the aisle. In some churches we can go up to the balcony and see the procession from up high. Let's pretend we are in the balcony and the Mass is ready to begin.

Craft Directions for Opening Procession (pages 35-38)

1. Use colored pencils or crayons to color the people in the processional and all or some of the people in the pews (pages 35 and 37).
2. Cut the two strips, A and B (page 37). Glue together as shown.
3. Carefully cut the dark lines around the people in the procession. (The teacher may wish to cut around the people with a razor or artist knife, allowing the children to fold the characters up. Several pages can be stacked and perforated at the same time. Or, instruct the children to fold the paper slightly at the slit and begin a small cut with the tip of the scissors. Then, cut away in both directions.)
4. Cut the slit in front of the altar. (The slit in front of the altar may be cut in the same manner as described in number 3.)
5. Slip the arrow part of the new long strip into the slit in front of the altar. Fold up the people on the strip on the dotted line.
6. Pull the strip and see the people "walk" up the aisle to the altar.
7. Fold the people down when not in use.

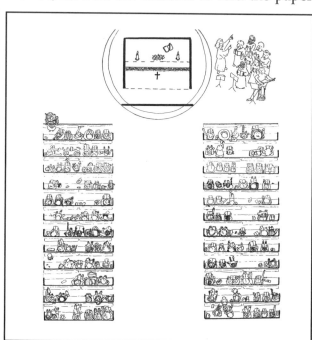

Review Questions

• Why do we stand and sing at the beginning of the Mass?
• Who is in the opening procession?
• What is the Lectionary?

Lesson 5:
Greeting

Background

We come from our homes and gather at Eucharist. As we do in any other social and communal setting, we greet one another as we greet Christ. We gather in the name of the Father, and of the Son, and of the Holy Spirit. This greeting may take place prior to the opening procession or after the priest has kissed the altar.

Say to the Students:

After the Sign of the Cross, the priest welcomes everyone to Mass. He asks that God's grace (friendship) be on all of us. We greet the priest and ask that God's blessings be on him too. We say, "And also with you." (Use the blank cards to fill in a different response if needed.)

Craft/Activity Directions for Greeting (pages 39-40)

1. Cut out the priest's greeting used most often at your parish's Sunday Mass or write a greeting on the blank card.
2. Glue the priest's greeting at the top of a half-sheet of colored paper.
3. Color the heart and cut out the heart *square* on the bold lines.
4. Glue left and right side and bottom of the heart square to the bottom of the half-sheet of colored paper.
5. Cut out the response cards "And also with you."
6. Ask someone to say the priest's greeting with you. Practice answering, "And also with you."
7. Each time you practice, color a small heart and slip it into the pocket.

Review Questions

- How do you greet someone when you welcome the person to your home?
- What words of greeting does the priest use?
- How do we respond to the priest's greeting?

Lesson 6:
Penitential Rite

Background

We come to church aware of our sins and shortcomings. The penitential rite helps us to confess our sorrow for any wrongdoing, knowing that God is there for us, ready to forgive.

Say to the Students:

We are called to be kind and understanding to one another. Sometimes we are careless or forget to treat others as we should. We are sorry. We want to tell God and our brothers and sisters of our sorrow before we listen to God's Word. In this prayer, we ask God to help us. We ask for blessings so that we will go out into the world acting as a holy people. God is always ready to forgive us. God's love is always there for us. We say (have the students recite along):

I confess to almighty God,
and to you, my brothers and sisters,
that I have sinned through my own fault
in my thoughts and in my words,
in what I have done,
and in what I have failed to do;
and I ask blessed Mary, ever virgin,
all the angels and saints,
and you, my brothers and sisters,
to pray for me to the Lord our God.

Craft/Activity Directions for Penitential Rite (pages 41-42)

1. Color the rebus pictures.
2. Ask someone to read the prayer with you.
3. Follow along and say the word represented by each picture.
4. Take the page with you to Mass and follow along when this prayer is said.

Review Questions

- When have you told someone you were sorry? How did you feel?
- How do you show God that you are sorry for things you do wrong?
- How do we know that God will always forgive us?

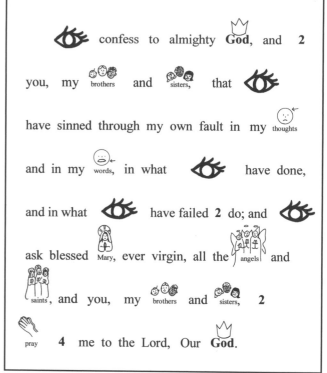

Lesson 7:
Lord, Have Mercy

Background

This is an ancient acclamation. In it we praise the Lord and implore his mercy. Sometimes this prayer is said in English, sometimes it is said in Greek. The "Lord, have mercy" itself may be used as the Penitential Rite.

Say to the Students:

Many years ago Greek was a commonly spoken language. So was Latin. The Mass was said in Latin. Part of it was also said in Greek. But times changed and people didn't speak Latin and Greek as much as they once did. Therefore, things were changed so that people now usually celebrate the Mass in their own languages. Still, it is good to remember the early church and the beautiful Greek and Latin languages. Sometimes the "Lord, have mercy" is sung, sometimes it is said. Sometimes it is said in Greek, sometimes it is said in English. Listen for the way it is said at a Mass you attend.

Craft/Activity Directions for Lord, Have Mercy (pages 43-44)

1. Trace in crayon the dotted lines of the Greek words.
2. Cut out the three rectangles.
3. Fold the rectangles on dotted lines with the words on the outside.
4. Cut a piece of yarn 12" to 15" long.
5. Glue the inside of the cards to the yarn so that the English is on one side and the Greek is on the other.
6. Tape the bottom of the yarn to a desktop. Turn the yarn and practice saying the prayer.

Review Questions

- What language is Kyrie eléison and Christe eléison?
- What does Kyrie eléison and Christe eléison mean?
- Why is the Mass mostly said in our own language now?

Lesson 8:
Glory to God

Background

The Glory to God is a joyous acclamation in which we praise God. We recognize the Father as our heavenly King and Jesus as the Lamb of God, our redeemer. We call on the Holy Spirit to be with us. We offer glory and praise. This prayer is not prayed during Advent and Lent. This is a joyous prayer that is most often sung.

Say to the Students:

In the Glory to God, we praise God in three persons, Father, Son, and Holy Spirit. Because this is a happy, joyous prayer we don't use it during Advent, the time of waiting for Jesus, or Lent, a time of penance and sorrow. When we do say this prayer it can be a loud, happy time with voices singing and bells and cymbals ringing. Sing out with joy! We say or sing (have the student recite along):

Glory to God in the highest, and peace to his people on earth.
Lord God, heavenly King, almighty God and Father,
we worship you, we give you thanks, we praise you for your glory.
Lord Jesus Christ, only Son of the Father, Lord God, Lamb of God,
you take away the sin of the world: have mercy on us;
you are seated at the right hand of the Father: receive our prayer.
For you alone are the Holy One, you alone are the Lord,
you alone are the Most High, Jesus Christ,
with the Holy Spirit, in the glory of God the Father. Amen.

Craft/Activity Directions for Glory to God (pages 45-46)

1. Color the drawings on the page.
2. Say the prayer.
3. Trace the underlined parts with a crayon or marker.
4. Repeat the prayer again with motions.
5. Try singing the prayer with motions while some children are ringing bells.

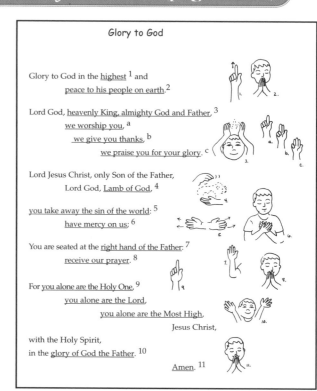

Glory to God

Glory to God in the <u>highest</u> [1] and
     <u>peace to his people on earth</u>.[2]

Lord God, <u>heavenly King, almighty God and Father</u>, [3]
     <u>we worship you</u>, [a]
          <u>we give you thanks</u>, [b]
               <u>we praise you for your glory</u>. [c]

Lord Jesus Christ, only Son of the Father,
     Lord God, <u>Lamb of God</u>, [4]

<u>you take away the sin of the world</u>: [5]
     <u>have mercy on us</u>; [6]

You are seated at the <u>right hand of the Father</u>: [7]
     <u>receive our prayer</u>. [8]

For <u>you alone are the Holy One</u>, [9]
     <u>you alone are the Lord</u>,
          <u>you alone are the Most High</u>,
               Jesus Christ,

with the Holy Spirit,
in the <u>glory of God the Father</u>. [10]

               <u>Amen</u>. [11]

Review Questions

- What does it mean to give glory to God?
- What times of the year is this prayer not said or sung at Mass?
- Why should this prayer be said with loud, happy voices?

We stand and sing during the *Opening Procession*.

We open our prayer in the name of the Father, and of the Son, and of the Holy Spirit. The music says, "Hello! Welcome!" We all stand and sing a song to begin Mass. Often there is a choir and the music is chosen just for Sunday's Mass. The altar servers, the lector and the priest walk up the aisle to the altar.

Name the people you see in the opening procession at Sunday Mass at your parish.

The Opening Procession

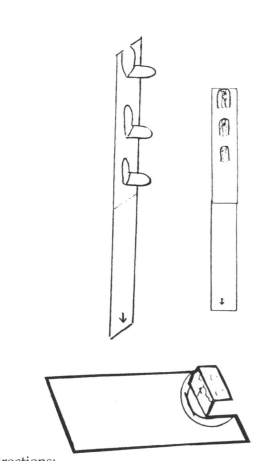

Directions:

1. Use colored pencils or crayons to color the people in the processional and all or some of the people in the pews (page 35).
2. Cut the two strips, A and B. Glue together as shown.
3. Carefully cut the dark lines around the people in the procession.
4. Cut the slit in front of the altar.
5. Slip the arrow part of the new long strip into the slit in front of the altar. Fold up the people on the strip on the dotted line.
6. Pull the strip and see the people "walk" up the aisle to the altar.
7. Fold the people down when not in use.

priest

lector

altar
servers

Lesson 4 Opening Procession

Greeting/Hearts "And Also with You" Cards

The grace of our Lord Jesus Christ and the love of God and the fellowship of the Holy Spirit be with you all.

The Lord be with you.

The grace and peace of God our Father and the Lord Jesus Christ be with you.

♡ And also with you.	♡ And also with you.
♡ And also with you.	♡ And also with you.
♡ And also with you.	♡ And also with you.
♡ And also with you.	♡ And also with you.
♡ And also with you.	♡ And also with you.
♡ And also with you.	♡ And also with you.

Directions:
1. Cut out the priest's greeting used most often at your parish's Sunday Mass or write a greeting on the blank card.
2. Glue the priest's greeting at the top of a half-sheet of colored paper.
3. Color the heart and cut out the heart *square* on the bold lines.
4. Glue left and right side and bottom of the heart square to the bottom of the half-sheet of colored paper.
5. Cut out the response cards "And also with you."
6. Ask someone to say the priest's greeting with you. Practice answering, "And also with you."
7. Each time you practice, color a small heart and slip it into the pocket.

- Color the back of each "And also with you" card.
- Stamp small hearts or stars on the back of the cards.
- Glue yarn around the border of the heart or heart pocket after it is glued to a colored sheet of paper.

Penitential Rite

(We are sorry for past wrong doings. God always forgives us and loves us.)

 confess to almighty **God**, and 2

you, my (brothers) and (sisters,) that

have sinned through my own fault in my (thoughts)

and in my (words,) in what  have done,

and in what  have failed 2 do; and

ask blessed (Mary,) ever virgin, all the (angels) and

(saints), and you, my (brothers) and (sisters,) 2

(pray) 4 me to the Lord, Our **God**.

Color the page. Practice the prayer. Take it to church with you and follow along.

- Roll up the page. Secure with a sticker or tie with a ribbon.
- Act out some of the words using motions such as pray (folded hands), I (point to your eye), thoughts (point to your forehead), and words (cup hands as if shouting).

Lord, have mercy, Kyrie eléison page

Lord, have mercy.	Kýrie, eléison.
Christ, have mercy.	Christe eléison.
Lord, have mercy.	Kýrie eléison.

Directions:
1. Trace in crayon the dotted lines of the Greek words.
2. Cut out the three rectangles.
3. Fold the rectangles on dotted lines with the words on the outside.
4. Cut a piece of yarn 12″ to 15″ long.
5. Glue the inside of the cards to the yarn so that the English is on one side and the Greek is on the other.
6. Tape the bottom of the yarn to a desktop. Turn the yarn and practice saying the prayer.

Optional:
- Trace the words on the cards.
- Cut out the cards.
- Fold on dotted lines to make V shapes.
- Stack the cards in the order they are said.
- Read and repeat.

Glory to God

Glory to God in the <u>highest</u> [1] and
    <u>peace to his people on earth</u>.[2]

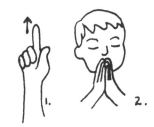

Lord God, <u>heavenly King, almighty God and Father</u>, [3]
    <u>we worship you</u>, [a]
        <u>we give you thanks</u>, [b]
            <u>we praise you for your glory</u>. [c]

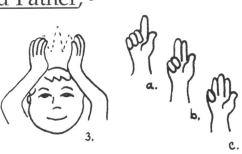

Lord Jesus Christ, only Son of the Father,
    Lord God, <u>Lamb of God</u>, [4]

<u>you take away the sin of the world</u>: [5]
    <u>have mercy on us</u>; [6]

You are seated at the <u>right hand of the Father</u>: [7]
    <u>receive our prayer</u>. [8]

For <u>you alone are the Holy One</u>, [9]
    <u>you alone are the Lord</u>,
        <u>you alone are the Most High</u>,
                Jesus Christ,

with the Holy Spirit,
in the <u>glory of God the Father</u>. [10]
                <u>Amen</u>.[11]

- Color the drawings on the page. Say the prayer. Trace the underlined parts with a crayon or marker. Repeat the prayer again with motions. Try singing the prayer with motions while some children are ringing bells.

- Roll up the page. Secure it with a sticker or tie it with a ribbon.
- Record your church choir singing the Glory to God. Play the music for the children and help them to perform the motions along with the music.

3

Liturgy of the Word

Lesson 9: Liturgy of the Word Sequence

Lesson 10: First Reading, Responsorial Psalm, Second Reading

Lesson 11: Preparing for the Gospel

Lesson 12: The Gospel

Lesson 13: Profession of Faith

Lesson 14: General Intercessions (Prayer of the Faithful)

Lesson 15: Our Gifts

Note: Lessons 9 to 12 may be combined into one session for older children. For younger children, combine Lessons 10 and 12 into one session, allowing Lesson 11 to be a focal point of a single session before or after this combined lesson.

Lesson 9:
Liturgy of the Word Sequence

Background

It is easier to understand the Liturgy of the Word if we "see" the parts. There is a sequential order to readings. The first reading is usually from the Old Testament and has a theme in common with the day's gospel. The second reading is from the New Testament letters. The Church also sequences the readings in larger cycles, A, B, and C, so that a larger portion of the scriptures may be heard over a three-year period.

Say to the Students:

The Bible is a wonderful book. It is divided into the Old Testament and the New Testament. In the first reading at Mass we listen to a reading from the Old Testament. We pray and think about that reading and sing a psalm that is also from the Old Testament. Then we share a second reading. This reading is usually from letters written by one of Jesus' friends, mostly St. Paul. Next, we sing a song of joy called the "alleluia" and stand for the gospel ("good news"). In the gospel, we welcome Jesus and hear his words.

Craft Directions for Liturgy of the Word Sequence (pages 55-56)

1. Lightly color the pieces. Then cut them out.
2. On a long strip of colored paper (4 1/4" x 11"), glue the books in order by size, starting with the smallest book at the top.
3. Glue the Responsorial Psalm and Alleluia between the books.

Review Questions

• Is the first reading usually from the Old Testament or New Testament?
• Who wrote most of the second readings?
• Is the gospel from the Old Testament or New Testament?

Lesson 10:

First Reading, Responsorial Psalm, Second Reading

Background

The lector is the person from the community of faith who reads from the Lectionary at Mass. The first reading is from the Old Testament, the second reading is from the New Testament. A psalm response is shared between the two readings. Practice the response to the first and second readings. Say, "The Word of the Lord" and ask the children to respond "Thanks be to God."

Say to the Students:

We pause to listen to the Word of God. The lector comes to the podium, called the lectern. First, he or she reads from the Old Testament. This is the first reading. Next, we sing or say a response to a prayer from the book of Psalms which is also from the Old Testament. Then we listen to a second reading. This special reading, usually a letter written by St. Paul or one of Jesus' other friends, helps us to understand more about God's love for us.

Craft Direction for First Reading, Responsorial Psalm, Second Reading (pages 57-58)

1. Color and cut out the lector, lectern (stand), and the Lectionary (book).
2. Fold the lectern on the dotted lines.
3. Cut and glue the stand to the back of the lector.
4. Glue the Lectionary on the "wooden" surface.
5. The lector may be male or female. Cut off the side curls for a male.

Review Questions

• What is the special name for the reader?
• How do we respond to the readings after the lector says "The Word of the Lord?"
• Is the lector a man or a woman?

Note: This same piece is used for Lesson 12, The Gospel. The priest cutout from that lesson is placed in front of the reader on the podium.

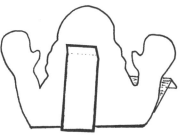

Lesson 11:
Preparing for the Gospel

Background

The "alleluia" is part of our preparation for the reading of the gospel. During Lent the alleluia is omitted and the gospel acclamation is said instead. The alleluia is a song of joy, a reminder that Jesus won for us our salvation. It has been included here with the preparation for the gospel since it needs to be introduced but not given a full lesson consideration. The preparation for the gospel is a key element to arrest our attention for the good news that is about to be proclaimed.

Say to the Students:

We stand and sing a song of joy. We sing "alleluia!" Then, we hear the good news of Jesus. The priest calls for the Lord to be with us, and we offer him the same greeting. He tells us that the gospel comes to us by Matthew, Mark, Luke, or John. These special disciples wrote the gospels. During the *Liturgy of the Word* we share these writings and God's own holy words. With our hand held closed like we are holding a precious stone and our thumb up like a little piece of chalk, we make three crosses. One cross is on our forehead, one cross is on our lips, one cross is over our heart. We can practice this and be ready for when we hear the priest announce the gospel in church.

Note: The teacher should model holding the hand like a fist with the thumb up and the making of the three Signs of Cross on forehead, lips, and heart.

Craft/Activity Directions for Preparing for the Gospel (pages 59-60)

1. Color the person on the worksheet.
2. Cut on the bold line and fold the arm on the dotted line.
3. Trace the three crosses with a pencil or crayon. Pray as you trace: "May these words be in our thoughts, on our lips, and in our hearts." Or, "May I hear the word of God, speak the word of God, and love the word of God."
4. Next, place a small candy on each cross. Say the words as you trace the crosses with your thumb. As you say each part, you may eat the candy.
5. Place a heart or cross sticker on each cross as you repeat the words.
6. Lastly, pray the words again as you cross yourself three times.

Review Questions

- What is the name of the song of joy we sing before the gospel?
- Why do we cross ourselves three times?
- What are the words that we say?

Lesson 12:
The Gospel

Background

The culmination of the Liturgy of the Word is the proclamation of the gospel and the sharing of the homily. Jesus Christ is manifested in the gospel. In the gospel, God's love for us is unmistakable, clear, and present. We follow the Lord Jesus as his ministry unfolds. Then, in the homily, the priest or deacon speaks to us and helps connect the gospel to our own experience. The relevancy of the gospel to our daily lives is revealed to us by listening and contemplating.

Say to the Students:

We listen to the reading from the gospel. Gospel means "good news" and what good news the gospel reading conveys. We can follow Jesus as he lived, taught and poured out God's love for us. We listen and can learn God's wonderful plan for us. We stand for the gospel as a sign of respect. We are so happy after hearing the gospel that we all say together, "Praise to You Lord, Jesus Christ!" Then, after the gospel, we sit and the priest shares special thoughts and ideas with us. This is called the homily. He helps us to love and practice the word of God.

Craft Directions for The Gospel (pages 61-62)

1. Color the priest.
2. Cut out the priest at the lectern.
3. Place the priest in front of the lector (see Lesson 10) or color, cut, and fold the optional lectern, Lectionary, and stand from this page if the lesson has been done separately.

Review Questions

- What does the word "gospel" mean?
- Why do we stand for the gospel?
- What is the homily?

Lesson 13:
Profession of Faith

Background

The Profession of Faith is our affirmation of our Catholic beliefs. We stand as a community and state our beliefs. To profess means to assert, declare, and "lay claim to." We are laying claim to our beliefs as a united people of God. While the children may not appreciate that over 1,500 years ago theologians gathered together in a town in Turkey named *Nicaea* and composed the basis for the Nicene Creed we say today, they can comprehend that this prayer has been passed down through time. In this lesson we present both the *Nicene Creed* which children will hear at most Masses and the shorter *Apostles' Creed*, which is often reserved for Masses with children in which only a few adults are present. With young children, a reading of the creed is meant to simply introduce and help establish initial awareness of our beliefs in succinct form.

Say to the Students:

When we feel strongly about something, we want to shout it out to everyone. After the good news of the gospel is shared with us, we stand and say our beliefs in a special prayer. This prayer is called the *Nicene Creed* and it was written over 1,500 years ago in a place called Nicaea. The creed is a prayer that tells what we believe. In this prayer, we also praise God. Sometimes, at Masses with only children present, we pray the *Apostles' Creed*. It is a bit shorter than the Nicene Creed. Its beginnings can be traced to the time of the apostles.

Craft/Activity Directions for Profession of Faith (pages 63-64)

1. Color the pictures around the edges of the creed.
2. As the prayer is read, trace the lines from the underlined words to the pictures.

Review Questions

- When and where was most of the Nicene Creed written?
- What is a creed?
- What are two things you say you believe in when you pray the creed?

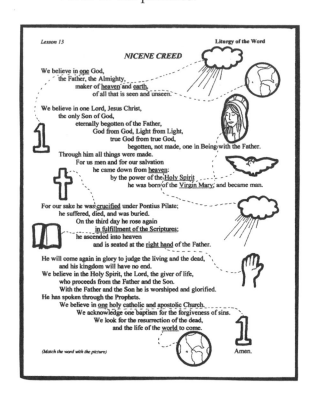

Lesson 14:
General Intercessions (Prayer of the Faithful)

Background

We pray for the needs of all the Church, living and dead. We ask for God's help for all of humanity. We call on God in petition to intercede in our lives with help and guidance. We incorporate the needs we see around us in our community as well as our personal desires. We thank God for the blessings received.

Say to the Students:

When we are at Mass we pray for the needs of all members of God's family. God listens to us as we pray. We can pray in our hearts for what we need. Is someone in your family sick? Ask God to bless the person. Do you feel especially happy about a gift from God you have received? At Mass, after we petition God with our prayers we say, "Lord, hear our prayer."

Note: Use the petition response most common to the child's service.

Craft/Activity Directions for Intercessions/Prayer of the Faithful (page 65-66)

1. Draw or write petitions on the lines. (Help the children put the petitions into verbal requests. Have them practice saying the petitions and responses.)
2. Incorporate the prayers of petition into a school Mass or share them with a family member.

Review Questions

- Why do we pray to God?
- How do you answer the prayer petition at Mass?
- Who is someone who needs your prayers right now?

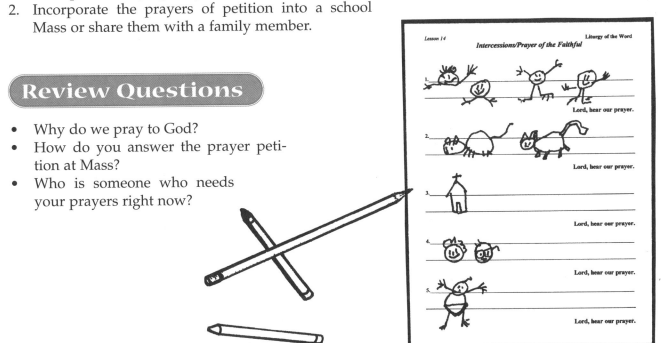

Lesson 15:
Our Gifts

Background

The practical aspects of the monetary collection provide for the upkeep of the church and required fiscal responsibilities. A monetary offering is one element of our call to be good stewards. Yet, children need to also realize that we have an active call to support the Church with our time and talents as well. The monetary collection is brought to the altar along with the unconsecrated bread and wine at the beginning of the Liturgy of the Eucharist. This presentation of our gifts is a good reference point for the children. As our gifts are taken to the altar we are now entering the most sacred part of the Mass, the Liturgy of the Eucharist.

Say to the Students:

When you go to a party, do you usually bring a gift? We bring gifts because it is a happy occasion and we want to share in the celebration. At the celebration of Mass we also bring gifts. A long time ago, gifts of food and drink were collected by the faithful as a support to those in need. Today, a basket is passed. We place money in the basket. In this way everyone can help to support the Church. It takes money to buy candles, instruments, books and music. Our money goes to the missions around the world. It helps to feed poor people in our own community. We thank God for all of our blessings. As we enter the Liturgy of the Eucharist our gifts are carried to the altar along with the bread and wine.

Craft Directions for Our Gifts (pages 67-68)

1. Color and cut out the basket front.
2. Fold the basket and glue the bottom and sides to form a carrying pouch.
3. Cut out the envelopes. Fold and tape as shown.
4. Color and cut out the money. Slip the money into the envelopes, then into the opening of the basket.

Review Questions

- Why do we bring our gifts of money to church?
- What else is carried to the altar along with our gifts of money?
- Have you ever been asked to carry the gifts to the altar?

Liturgy of the Word Sequence

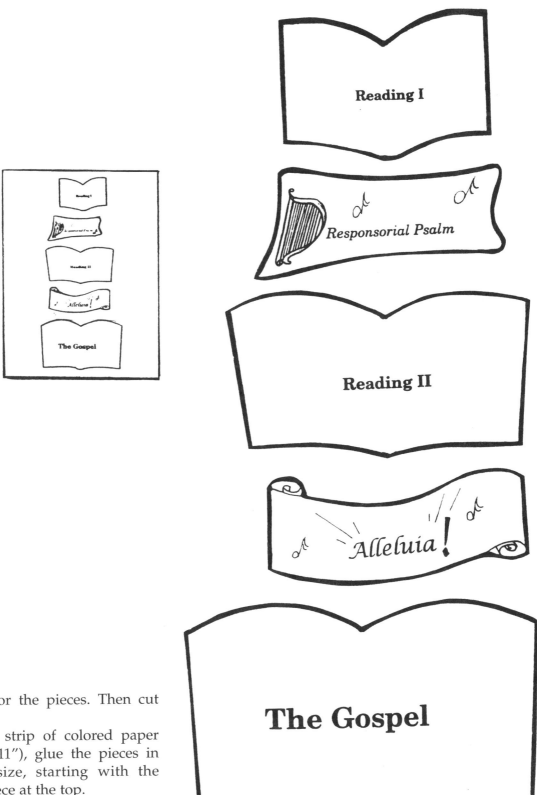

Reading I

Responsorial Psalm

Reading II

Alleluia!

The Gospel

Directions:
1. Lightly color the pieces. Then cut them out.
2. On a long strip of colored paper (4 1/4" x 11"), glue the pieces in order by size, starting with the smallest piece at the top.

Cut out this card. Laminate. Keep the card to help you to remember the sequence of the Liturgy of the Word. Or, glue it to the back of the Liturgy of the Word sequence page that you made.

First Reading This reading comes from the Old Testament. Its theme is in common with the gospel.

Responsorial Psalm This song or prayer comes from the Book of Psalms, some of which was written by King David.

Second Reading This reading often comes from letters of the apostles—mostly St. Paul.

Alleluia! This is a happy song of praise to God we sing to welcome the gospel.

The Gospel This is a reading from the New Testament books of Matthew, Mark, Luke, or John. Jesus is present to us in the gospels.

Thank you, God, for your words of love!

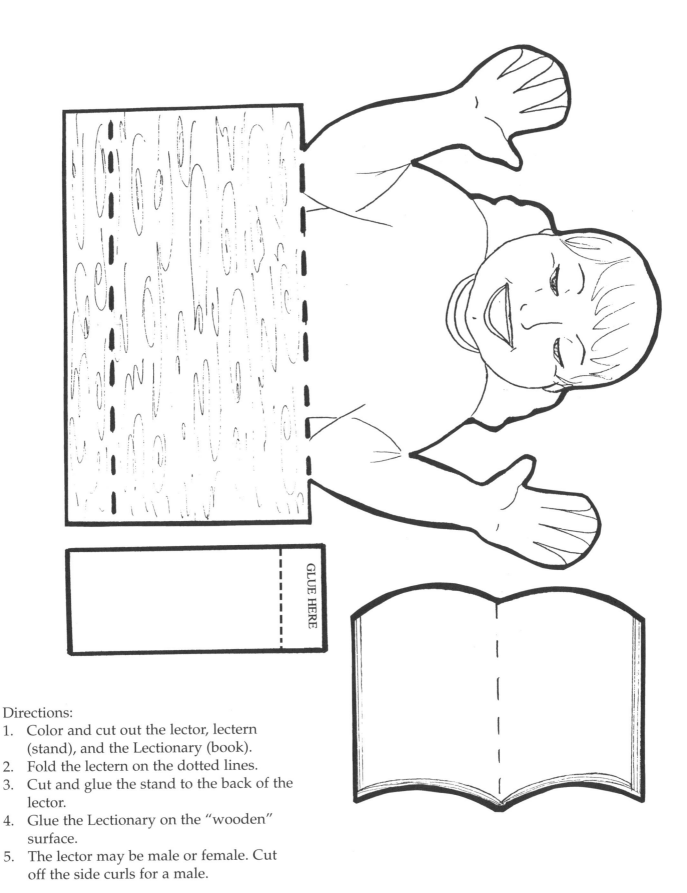

GLUE HERE

Directions:
1. Color and cut out the lector, lectern (stand), and the Lectionary (book).
2. Fold the lectern on the dotted lines.
3. Cut and glue the stand to the back of the lector.
4. Glue the Lectionary on the "wooden" surface.
5. The lector may be male or female. Cut off the side curls for a male.

Glue stand to the
back of the lector here.

The lector is a reader. The lector
reads from a book called the
Lectionary.

Lectionary

Preparing for the Gospel

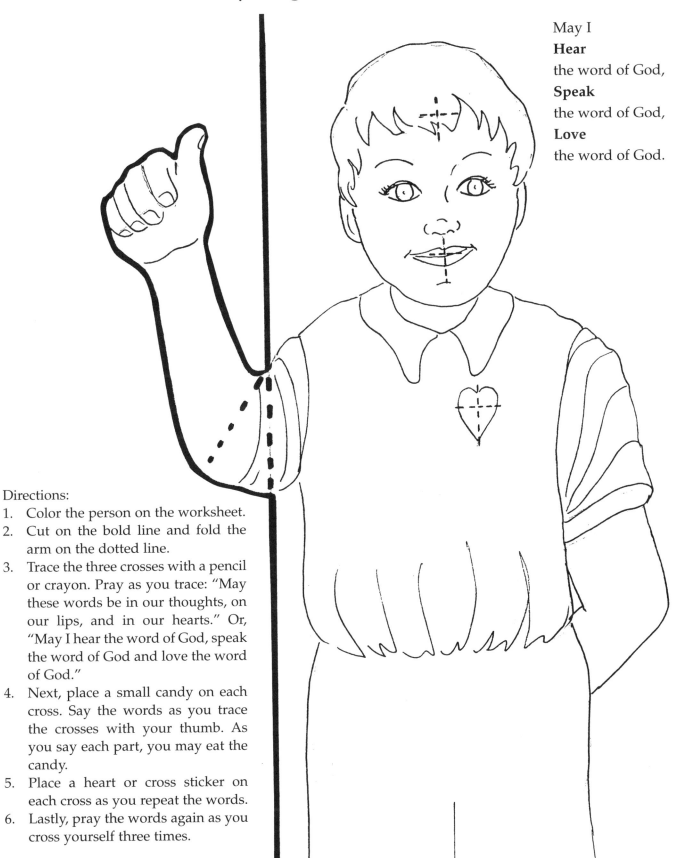

May I
Hear
the word of God,
Speak
the word of God,
Love
the word of God.

Directions:

1. Color the person on the worksheet.
2. Cut on the bold line and fold the arm on the dotted line.
3. Trace the three crosses with a pencil or crayon. Pray as you trace: "May these words be in our thoughts, on our lips, and in our hearts." Or, "May I hear the word of God, speak the word of God and love the word of God."
4. Next, place a small candy on each cross. Say the words as you trace the crosses with your thumb. As you say each part, you may eat the candy.
5. Place a heart or cross sticker on each cross as you repeat the words.
6. Lastly, pray the words again as you cross yourself three times.

May I
Hear
the word of God,

Speak
the word of God,

Love
the word of God.

The Gospel
(Priest or Deacon)

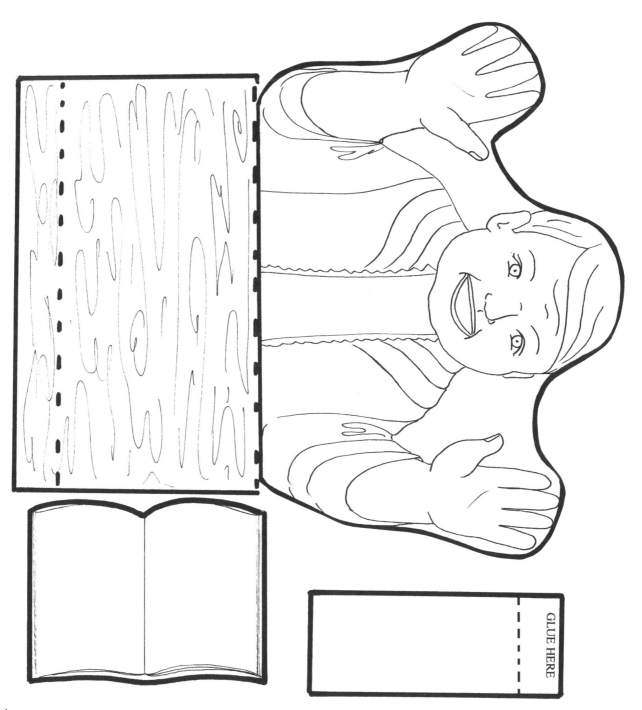

GLUE HERE

Directions:
1. Color the priest.
2. Cut out the priest at the lectern.
3. Place the priest in front of the lector (see Lesson 10) or color, cut, and fold the optional lectern, Lectionary, and stand from this page if the lesson has been done separately.

Glue the stand to back of priest here.

The priest reads the gospel and then talks with us and explains the gospel and other readings in the homily.

If the Lesson 10 lectern is used as a separate lesson, cut and fold the new lectern from page 61. Glue the stand to the back of the priest.

NICENE CREED

We believe in one God,
   the Father, the Almighty,
      maker of heaven and earth,
         of all that is seen and unseen.

We believe in one Lord, Jesus Christ,
   the only Son of God,
      eternally begotten of the Father,
         God from God, Light from Light,
            true God from true God,
               begotten, not made, one in Being with the Father.

Through him all things were made.
   For us men and for our salvation
      he came down from heaven:
         by the power of the Holy Spirit
            he was born of the Virgin Mary, and became man.

For our sake he was crucified under Pontius Pilate;
   he suffered, died, and was buried.
On the third day he rose again
   in fulfillment of the Scriptures;
      he ascended into heaven
         and is seated at the right hand of the Father.

He will come again in glory to judge the living and the dead,
   and his kingdom will have no end.
We believe in the Holy Spirit, the Lord, the giver of life,
   who proceeds from the Father and the Son.
   With the Father and the Son he is worshiped and glorified.
He has spoken through the Prophets.
   We believe in one holy catholic and apostolic Church.
      We acknowledge one baptism for the forgiveness of sins.
         We look for the resurrection of the dead,
            and the life of the world to come.

   Amen.

Color the pictures. Match the word with the picture.

APOSTLES' CREED

I believe in God, the Father almighty,
    creator of heaven and earth.
I believe in Jesus Christ, his only Son, our Lord.
    He was conceived by the power of the Holy Spirit
        and born of the Virgin Mary.
    He suffered under Pontius Pilate,
        was crucified, died, and was buried.
    He descended to the dead.
    On the third day he rose again.
    He ascended into heaven,
        and is seated at the right hand of the Father.
    He will come again to judge the living and the dead.
I believe in the Holy Spirit,
    the holy catholic Church,
    the communion of saints,
    the forgiveness of sins,
    the resurrection of the body,
        and life everlasting.   Amen.

Sometimes we say the Apostles' Creed instead of the Nicene Creed. The words are similar. This prayer is a little shorter and sometimes used in a children's Mass.

Intercessions
(Prayer of the Faithful)

1. _____

   _____

   Lord, hear our prayer.

2. _____

   _____

   Lord, hear our prayer.

3. _____

   _____

   Lord, hear our prayer.

4. _____

   _____

   Lord, hear our prayer.

5. _____

   _____

   Lord, hear our prayer.

After the Intercessions (Prayer of the Faithful) the priest offers a concluding prayer and once more we say:

- Color the Amen.
- Draw faces around the Amen to show the people in the church.

Our Gifts

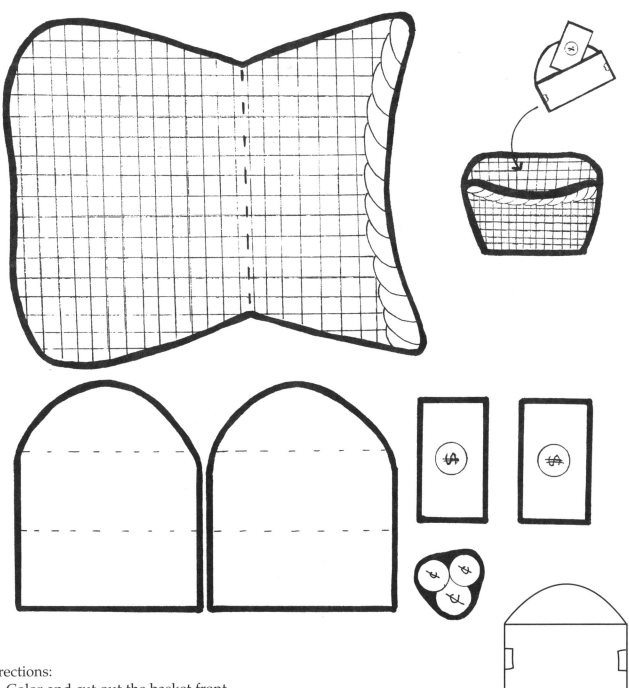

Directions:
1. Color and cut out the basket front.
2. Fold the basket and glue the bottom and sides to form a carrying pouch.
3. Cut out the envelopes. Fold and tape as shown.
4. Color and cut out the money. Slip the money into the envelopes, then into the opening of the basket.

Our Gifts

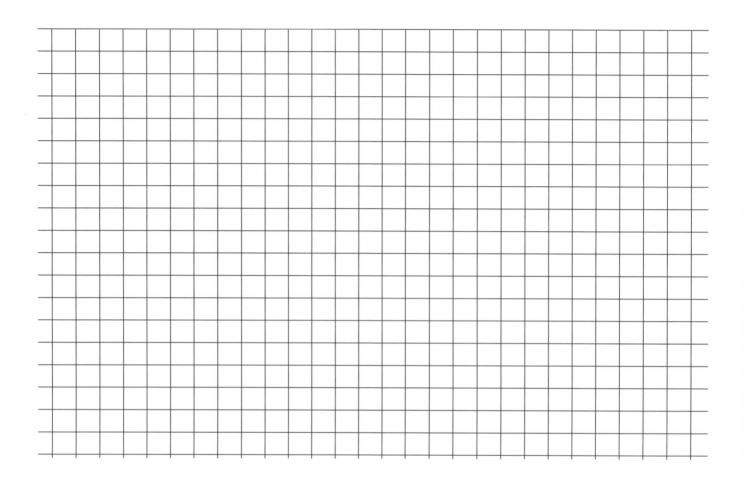

4

Liturgy of the Eucharist

Lesson 16: Liturgy of the Eucharist Sequence

Lesson 17: Preparation, Prayer, Dialogue

Lesson 18: Holy, Holy, Holy

Lesson 19: Consecration

Lesson 20: Memorial Acclamation

Lesson 21: The Great Amen

Lesson 22: The Lord's Prayer

Lesson 23: Sign of Peace

Lesson 24: Lamb of God

Lesson 25: Communion

Lesson 26: Prayer After Communion

Lesson 16:
Liturgy of the Eucharist Sequence

Background

As with the Liturgy of the Word, there is also a sequential order to the Liturgy of the Eucharist. First, the gifts are prepared. Then, they are blessed. Next, we come together in a shared communion to eat and drink the body and blood of Christ.

Say to the Students:

Many things take place during the Liturgy of the Eucharist. Sometimes we can better understand what happens if we can see the order in which they take place.

Just like at home, your family prepares food. When the food is ready, it is shared. We take food into our bodies to make us stronger and help us to grow. In the same manner, the bread and wine are prepared, blessed, and shared to make us grow stronger in God's love. At home, we clear the table when the meal is finished, much as we clear the church altar. Lastly, at home we share and visit with our families after we eat just as we go forth from church to share our love of God.

Craft Directions for Liturgy of the Eucharist Sequence (pages 81-82)

1. Color and cut out the four squares.
2. On a long strip of colored paper, glue the pieces in sequential order.

Review Questions

- How does a family meal you have shared remind you of the Mass?
- What can you do to pay better attention during Mass?
- How do you share God's love after you leave Mass?

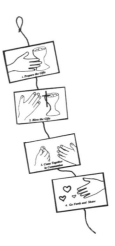

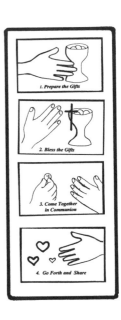

Lesson 17:
Preparation, Prayer, Dialogue

Background

The eucharistic prayer is a dialogue between the priest and people. The eucharistic prayer begins with introductory dialogue. The priest offers that the Lord is with us and we respond, "And also with you." The priest then reminds us to lift up our hearts. We agree by responding, "We lift them up to the Lord." Lastly the priest reminds us that we are giving thanks. Again, we affirm, "It is right to give him thanks and praise." These words are said so automatically that we may say them without considering their importance. Children, called on to listen and say the response for the first time, should realize that we are active participants in the Eucharist, and that the dialogue between priest and people continues through the Great Amen.

Say to the Students:

Most of us like to talk. Talking helps us to share ideas and interests. Talking helps us to let people know how we feel and what we think. If you have ever watched a little brother or sister just learning to talk, you know that words you want them to learn have to be repeated over and over again. You repeat the word, and then, one day you realize that he or she now knows how to say it. It is important for people to talk and share. In this part of the Mass, the priest talks to us and we answer back. The priest says: "The Lord be with you." We say: "And also with you." The priest says: "Lift up your hearts." We say: "We lift them up to the Lord." The priest says: "Let us give thanks to the Lord our God." We say: "It is right to give him thanks and praise."

Craft/Activity Directions for Preparation, Prayer, Dialogue (pages 83-84)

1. Read the prayers and dialogue aloud.
2. Cut out the various puzzle cards.
3. Match the "Priest says" cards to the "We say" cards.
4. Glue the cards in place on colored paper.

Note: If you prefer, after cutting have the students place the pieces in an envelope. They may take them home with the page to use as a puzzle.

Review Questions

- What is good about talking and listening?
- How can we help to prepare the gifts at Mass?
- How can we learn how to answer the priest at Mass?

Lesson 18:

Holy, Holy, Holy

Background

Hosanna is a cry of acclamation and adoration. While the Eucharist calls us to recall the sacrifice Jesus made for us all, it calls on us to affirm our redemption. Therefore, the Eucharist brings us great joy. We are redeemed by his body and blood. Our joy is evident. We praise God's power, might and glory. We call out in a happy voice, "Hosanna!" Hosanna is a cry of acclamation and adoration.

Say to the Students:

When we go to a party or event that makes us happy, we want to sing out and cheer. We wave flags and balloons, sing songs and play musical instruments. At this part of the Mass we praise God with all the angels. *Hosanna* is a Hebrew word that means *pray* or *save (us)*! We are so happy that we sing or say:

> Holy, holy, holy
> Lord, God of power and might.
> Heaven and earth are full of your glory.
> Hosanna in the highest.
> Blessed is he who comes in the name of the Lord.
> Hosanna in the highest.

Craft/Activity Directions for Holy, Holy, Holy (pages 85-86)

1. Color or paint the Hosanna! and Holy, Holy, Holy flags. Then cut them out.
2. Tape or glue the flags to straws or craft sticks.
3. Sing or say the Holy, Holy, Holy! while waving the flags. Or, play musical instruments (cymbals, triangles, drums) to accompany the singing.

Review Questions

- When are times we wave flags and sing?
- What does *Hosanna* mean?
- Why are we so happy when we think about Jesus?

Lesson 19:

Consecration

Background

The consecration is the most important part of the Liturgy of the Eucharist, but also the most difficult part to explain to children. The *epiclesis* is the invocation where the priest (with us) invokes God's power and asks that our gifts be consecrated to become the body and blood of Christ. The priest calls on God's power by saying: "(God) let your Spirit come upon these gifts to make them holy, so that they may become for us the body and blood of our Lord, Jesus Christ." It is sufficient that young children come to appreciate the solemnity of this portion of the Mass and to understand that we have been dictated by the Lord to share in the sacrifice. We serve as an example to children by keeping our eyes on the altar during the consecration, avoiding distractions. A simple motion, such as a finger to the lips, reminds children that this is a quiet time. Children should be given a good vantage point so they can see, hear, and appreciate the attention given to the prayers and solemnity of the consecration.

Say to the Students:

The time of the Mass where the priest repeats the words and actions of Jesus at the Last Supper is called the *consecration*. We should be very quiet, respectful, and listen carefully to the priest. At the Last Supper, Jesus blessed and broke bread and shared it with his disciples (friends). Then, he took a cup of wine and blessed and shared it. Jesus said, "Do this in memory of me."

The priest blesses the bread and holds it up for all to see. Next, he blesses the cup and holds it up for all to see. He may bow or genuflect after doing these things. This is the most special time during the Mass. We look and listen quietly as the priest raises the host and chalice. We think of the Last Supper when Jesus told his disciples he would always be present in the bread and wine.

Craft/Activity Directions for Consecration (pages 87-88):

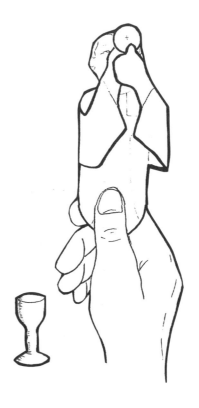

1. Color the priest, host, and chalice.
2. Cut out all of the pieces.
3. Fold the priest's arms.
4. Tape the host in the priest's hands; lift the priest high.
5. Repeat with the chalice.

Note: Provide a small envelope for each child so that the pieces can easily be transported home.

Review Questions

- What do we call the special meal in which Jesus shared bread and wine with his friends?
- Why does the priest hold up the host and chalice? What does he say when he does these things?
- Why do we stay quiet and look at the priest during this part of the Mass?

Lesson 20:
Memorial Acclamation

Background

The Memorial Acclamation reminds us of the mystery of faith. The *anamnesis* (memorial acclamation) is a "calling to mind" where we remember the Lord's death, resurrection, and ascension. We are thankful for "this holy and living sacrifice." We share a prayer and response. Along with the prayer, we see the risen Lord, overcoming death and ascending in glory. The symbolism of the staff (Jesus is shepherd), lily (triumph over death) and the rays (glory of the resurrection) serve as visuals for the Memorial Acclamation. We are invited to share this prayer. It is three short lines that sum up God's love for us. (Choose the one most appropriate for your children's level of understanding.)

Say to the Students:

After the consecration, we say a prayer that helps us to remember Christ's death, resurrection, and ascension. We see the risen Lord in glory overcoming death. Jesus died for us, and therefore, saved us. The priest or deacon says: "Let us proclaim the mystery of faith." We say one of the following:

Christ has died, Christ is risen, Christ will come again.

Dying you destroyed our death, rising you restored our life. Lord Jesus, come in glory.

When we eat this bread and drink this cup, we proclaim your death, Lord Jesus, until you come in glory.

Lord, by your cross and resurrection you have set us free. You are the Savior of the world.

Craft/Activity Directions for Memorial Acclamation (pages 89-90)

1. Color or paint the picture.
2. Glue colored glitter to the rays.
3. Write one or more of the acclamations on the back of the page.

Review Questions

• Who did Jesus die for?
• What does it mean to say that you believe you will see Jesus again?
• What is a mystery of faith?

Memorial Acclamation
(Remembering the Resurrection)
During this part of the Mass, we are reminded of Jesus' sacrifice for us by His dying on the cross and His promise fulfilled by His rising from the dead.

Lesson 21:
The Great Amen

Background

Remember, the eucharistic prayer is dialogue. We confirm our agreement for what we have heard and experienced by responding to a final doxology with a "Great Amen." The children should realize that our active participation in the Mass is again affirmed in this small but powerful prayer that reminds us that all glory and honor belong to the Lord, and that all things come through him, with him, and in him in the unity of the Holy Spirit.

Say to the Students:

What we say and do is an important part of the Mass. After the bread and wine are blessed we want to show that we are happy and understand what has taken place. We know that all things come from God. We stand and say or sing only one word, but that word is a very important one. We say a Hebrew word that means "Yes! We agree! Right!" That word is *amen*. This amen is a very special one. Sometimes it is called "the Great Amen."

The priest holds up the bread and wine and prays: "Through him, with him, in him, in the unity of the Holy Spirit, all glory and honor is yours, almighty Father, for ever and ever."

We call or sing out loudly with a wonderful "Amen!"

Craft Directions for The Great Amen (pages 91-92)

1. Color or paint all or some of the Amen patterns.
2. Cut out the Amen patterns. Print a new "Amen" on the back of each pattern.
3. Make more Amen patterns of your own on colored paper shapes.
4. Punch a hole as indicated on each Amen pattern.
5. Use thread or string to hang the Amen patterns from a coat hanger or a loop of yarn.

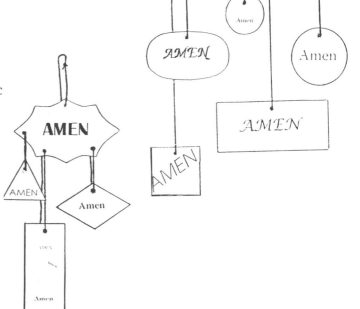

Review Questions

- What does *amen* mean in Hebrew?
- Why is the amen said after the eucharistic prayer called "the Great Amen?"
- What does the priest hold up when we say or sing the Great Amen?

Lesson 22:
The Lord's Prayer

Background

The Lord's Prayer is part of the Communion Rite. We are preparing to come to the altar to receive holy communion. We say a prayer that was given us by Jesus (Luke 11). By reciting the Lord's Prayer as one body (usually while holding hands) we petition God the Father for our daily bread. We ask for forgiveness from sin as we forgive others who "trespass against us." Too, we ask God's help in avoiding the test of evil. This prayer signifies our communion with God and the fellowship we share with one another.

Say to the Students:

Jesus taught his friends how to pray. This prayer is the Lord's Prayer or Our Father. When we say this prayer, just before communion, we pray together as a community. We hold hands to show that we are one family in Christ. As we say these holy words, think closely about their meaning and about the one who gave these words to us:

Our Father, who art in heaven, hallowed (holy or blessed) be thy name: thy kingdom come; thy will be done on earth as it is in heaven. Give us this day our daily bread; and forgive us our trespasses (wrong doing) as we forgive those who trespass against us; and lead us not into temptation (something or someone that tries to get us to do hurtful things), but deliver (lead) us from evil.

The priest adds: "Deliver us, Lord, from every evil, and grant us peace in our day. In your mercy keep us free from sin and protect us from all anxiety as we wait in joyful hope for the coming of our Savior, Jesus Christ."

Then, we conclude the prayer with: "For the kingdom, the power and the glory are yours, now and forever."

Note: Briefly explain the meaning of the words *hallowed, trespass, temptation* and *deliver* in words the students can comprehend. Parenthesis notes serve as an aid. Also, read the passage from Luke 11:1-4.

Craft/Activity Directions for The Lord's Prayer (pages 93-95)

1. Cut page in half on bold centerline.
2. Fold the right piece on the dotted lines accordion style.
3. Hold the folded piece closed with a paper clip. Then cut out the figure on the bold lines.
4. Open and unfold paper dolls.
5. Trim the shirt and hair for the second and fourth figures to make a girl-boy pattern.
6. Decorate.
7. Glue the hand of the first "paper doll" to the boy's hand at "X."
8. Practice saying The Lord's Prayer as you hold the people folded out.
9. Fold and paper clip dolls for storage.

Review Questions

- Who taught us the words to the Lord's Prayer?
- Why do we often hold hands to say this prayer?
- What is a word or phrase in the Our Father that you do not understand?

Lesson 23:

Sign of Peace

Background

At the Sign of Peace we offer both words and gestures—usually a handshake—to one another. This is another outward sign of our unity and love for one another. Beyond the physical sign, we are suggesting fellowship and peace to all God's children and reminding ourselves to be peacemakers in the world.

Say to the Students:

The Sign of Peace is a special time when we show that we are a big family in Jesus. When you shake hands with people around you, you should remember that you are sharing God's love, and that you should bring God's love and peace to all you meet.

The priest offers us Christ's peace. We offer it back to him. The priest asks us to share a sign of Christ's peace with others. The exchange goes like this:

Priest: Lord Jesus Christ, you said to your apostles: I leave you peace, my peace I give you. Look not on our sins, but on the faith of your Church, and grant us the peace and unity of your kingdom where you live for ever and ever.

We say: Amen.

Priest: The peace of the Lord be with you always.

We say: And also with you.

Priest or Deacon: Let us offer each other the sign of peace.

Craft Directions for Sign of Peace (pages 95-98)

1. Color the hands different shades of skin color (e.g. red, brown, peach, black, yellow). Or make copies of the hands on different colors of paper.
2. Cut out the hands.
3. Glue the hands on page 97, two at a time, to appear as if they are shaking hands in the Sign of Peace. (You will have to make separate copies of page 95.)

Optional: Make copies of and cut out a second set of hands. Make a "circle of love" wreath out of the hands and glue to page 98. Add a pair of hands by tracing your own.

Review Questions

- Why do we call this time the Sign of Peace?
- What do you say to people when you shake their hands?
- How can you share peace with others outside of Mass?

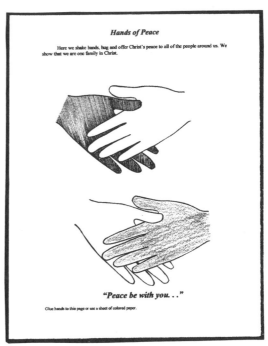

Hands of Peace

Here we shake hands, hug and offer Christ's peace to all of the people around us. We show that we are one family in Christ.

"Peace be with you. . ."

Glue hands to this page or use a sheet of colored paper.

Lesson 24:
Lamb of God

Background

In the Eucharist, we share Christ's body, broken that it can become one. At the Last Supper it can be assumed that Jesus took a large loaf of bread, blessed it, broke it and offered it to the disciples. Today, we use a more practical large host and small hosts. Still, after the priest breaks the large host, he holds it aloft in its broken form. This reminds us of Jesus' "breaking of the bread" at the Last Supper. It reminds us that Christ was "broken," blessed, and offered as a sacrifice to take away the sins of the world.

Say to the Students:

Christ is called the Lamb of God because he willingly died on the cross for our sins. Christ rose from the dead in glory. We think of this beautiful image of Christ. We say a special prayer at this time calling Jesus the *Lamb of God*. We say:

Lamb of God, you take away the sins of the world, have mercy on us.
Lamb of God, you take away the sins of the world, have mercy on us.
Lamb of God, you take away the sins of the world, grant us peace.

Craft/Activity Directions for Lamb of God (pages 99-100)

1. Color, paint or glue glitter to decorate the background.
2. Glue cotton balls on the body of the lamb to add texture.
3. Practice the response, "Lamb of God. . . ."

Review Questions

• Why is Jesus called the Lamb of God?
• What did Jesus take away by dying on the cross for us?
• How can the Lamb of God "have mercy on us" and "grant us peace?"

Note: Combine Lessons 24 and 25 to help the children see more clearly how the Lamb of God relates to the actual form of receiving communion.

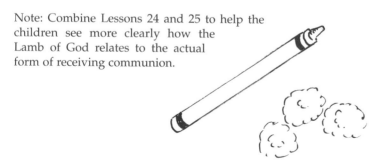

Lamb of God
(We are reminded that Jesus died for us and is called the Lamb of God.)

Lamb of God, you take away the sins of the world, have mercy on us.
Lamb of God, you take away the sins of the world, have mercy on us.
Lamb of God, you take away the sins of the world, grant us peace.

Directions:
1. Color, paint or decorate the background.
2. Glue pulled cotton balls on the body to add texture.
3. Reread the response, "Lamb of God . . ."

Lesson 25:
Communion

Background

At communion time, we have the joy of sharing the body and blood of Jesus Christ in the forms of bread and wine. Communion means to share, to come together. We know that God is great and loves us. Again, the Lamb of God reference is addressed in the general acclamation as we respond and ask to be made worthy to receive the Eucharist.

Say to the Students:

Those who have prepared for and received their first communion, now come forward to share the Eucharist. The priest holds up the host and chalice and says, "This is the Lamb of God who takes away the sins of the world. Happy are those who are called to his supper." We say, "Lord, I am not worthy to receive you, but only say the word and I shall be healed." Then, as the priest or eucharistic minister holds up a host to each person, he or she says: "The body of Christ." We respond: "Amen."

We come forward and receive communion with the whole community. But, after we return to our seats, we kneel and have a quiet time of prayer alone for a few moments. We think about the wonderful gift we just received and thank God for the love we share.

Craft Directions for Communion (pages 101-102)

1. Color and cut both the priest and the eucharistic minister cutouts.
2. Add these cutouts to the Mass scene from Lesson 3, Preparing for Mass.

Review Questions

- Why are we happy to be called to supper with the Lord?
- What does a eucharistic minister do?
- Why is it good for us to come back to our seats and have a few moments of quiet time after receiving communion?

Lesson 26:
Prayer After Communion

Background

After communion, the eucharistic ministers place any remaining blessed hosts in the tabernacle. The chalices are cleaned. For a moment the priest sits in reflection as we sit or kneel quietly preparing for the final prayer and blessing. Then, the priest, either sitting or standing, offers a closing prayer.

Say to the Students:

After everyone has gone to communion, the altar is cleared. The eucharistic ministers make sure that the blessed hosts are put away safely. Then, they return to their seats and the priest, after some quiet prayer of his own, offers a final prayer after communion. He begins, "Let us pray. . . ." We respond to the prayer, "Amen."

Following the prayer after communion, helpers in church might tell about upcoming events, read from the church bulletin, or remind people of something special that is taking place at parish. We often see people leave before this final prayer and the blessing. Just like at a party or celebration of any kind, it is not good to leave before the event is over. We should hear what the priest or a helper has to say about other things happening in the community. We should want the final blessing and we should be happy to sing a final song of glory to God. Out of respect and honor, we should stay until the priest has left the altar and walks down the aisle. It is good to give the Lord our full attention for the entire Mass.

Note: There is no craft to accompany Lesson 26. Ideally, Lesson 26 should be discussed with the students after Lesson 25. If this is not possible, allow Lesson 26 to serve as an introduction to Lesson 27, Final Blessing, in the Concluding Rite of the Mass.

Review Questions

- What happens to the unused blessed hosts after communion?
- What are some announcements you have heard by a priest or helper after communion?
- When should you leave Mass?

Liturgy of the Eucharist Sequence

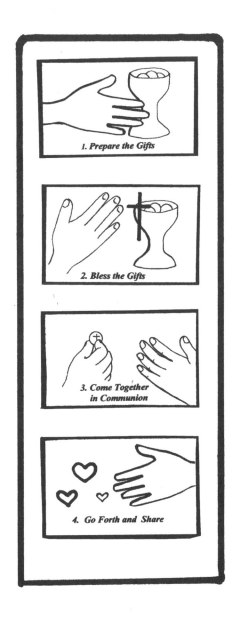

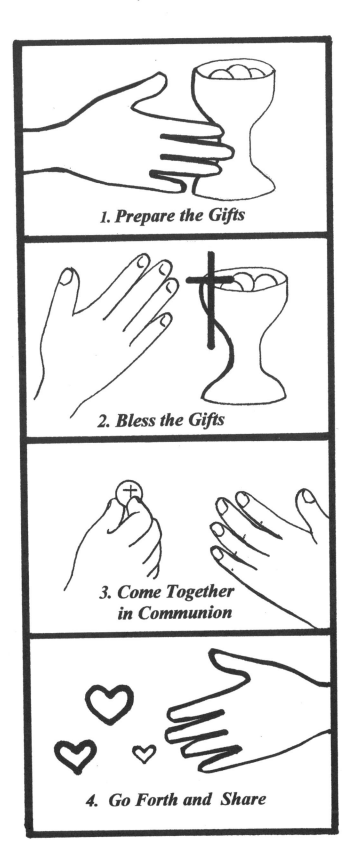

Directions:
1. Color and cut out the four squares.
2. On a long strip of colored paper, glue the pieces in sequential order.

Prepare the Gifts

Bless the Gifts

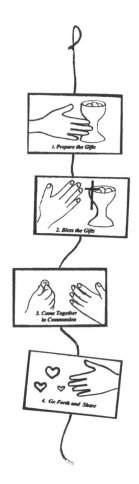

*Come Together
in Communion*

Go Forth and Share

Tape the pieces to yarn
in sequential order.

Preparation, Prayer, Dialogue

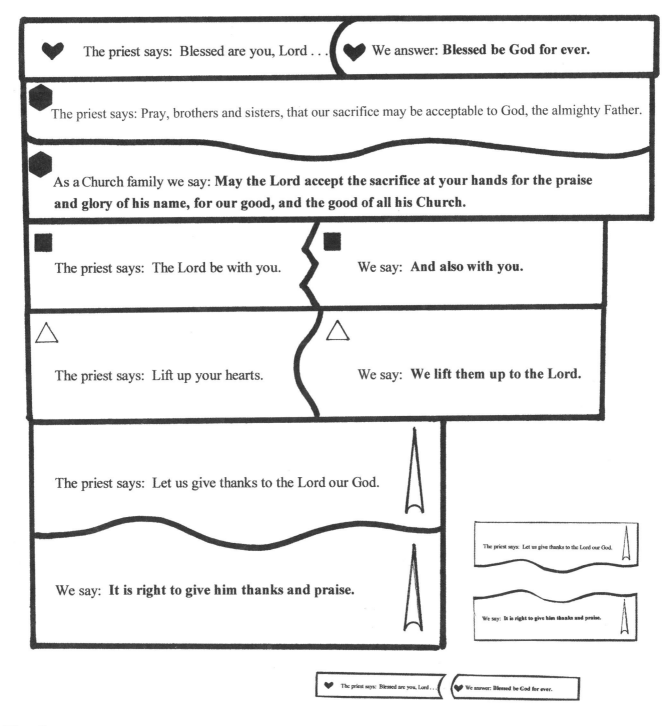

The priest says: Blessed are you, Lord . . .   We answer: **Blessed be God for ever.**

The priest says: Pray, brothers and sisters, that our sacrifice may be acceptable to God, the almighty Father.

As a Church family we say: **May the Lord accept the sacrifice at your hands for the praise and glory of his name, for our good, and the good of all his Church.**

The priest says: The Lord be with you.   We say: **And also with you.**

The priest says: Lift up your hearts.   We say: **We lift them up to the Lord.**

The priest says: Let us give thanks to the Lord our God.

We say: **It is right to give him thanks and praise.**

The priest says: Let us give thanks to the Lord our God.

We say: **It is right to give him thanks and praise.**

The priest says: Blessed are you, Lord . . .   We answer: Blessed be God for ever.

Directions:
1. Read the prayers and dialogue aloud.
2. Cut out the various puzzle cards.
3. Match the "Priest says" cards to the "We say" cards.
4. Glue the cards in place on colored paper.

- Color the cards. Make small decorated boxes or baskets to hold the dialogue cards.
- Write the response on the back of the card also. Or, choose one word from the response card and write it on the back.

Holy, Holy, Holy!

Hosanna!

Holy, Holy, Holy!

Directions:
1. Color or paint the Hosanna! and Holy, Holy, Holy flags. Then cut them out.
2. Tape or glue the flags to straws or craft sticks.
3. Sing or say the Holy, Holy, Holy! while waving the flags. Or, play musical instruments (cymbals, triangles, drums) to accompany the singing.

Holy, Holy, Holy!

Hosanna!

Holy, holy, holy Lord, God of power and might.
Heaven and earth are full of your glory. Hosanna in the highest.
Blessed is he who comes in the name of the Lord.
Hosanna in the highest.

Consecration

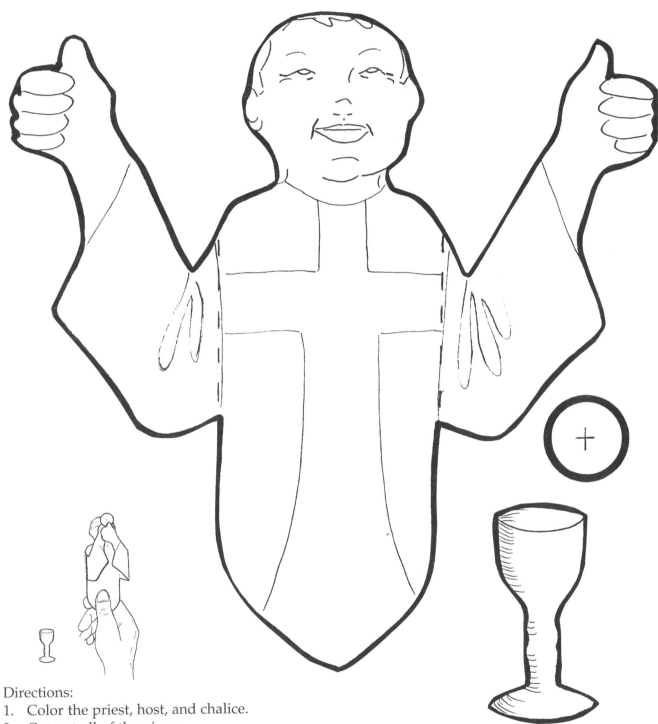

Directions:
1. Color the priest, host, and chalice.
2. Cut out all of the pieces.
3. Fold the priest's arms.
4. Tape the host in the priest's hands; lift the priest high.
5. Repeat with the chalice.

The priest holds up the host and chalice.
We remember the Last Supper and the sacrifice Jesus
made for all of us.

Memorial Acclamation
(Remembering the Resurrection)

During this part of the Mass, we are reminded of Jesus' sacrifice for us by his death on the cross and his promise fulfilled in his resurrection.

Color or paint the picture. Glue glitter to the rays.

Print or write the Memorial Acclamation that you use most often at your church:

_____

_____

_____

_____

_____

Write one or more of the Memorial Acclamations on the lines above.

The Great Amen

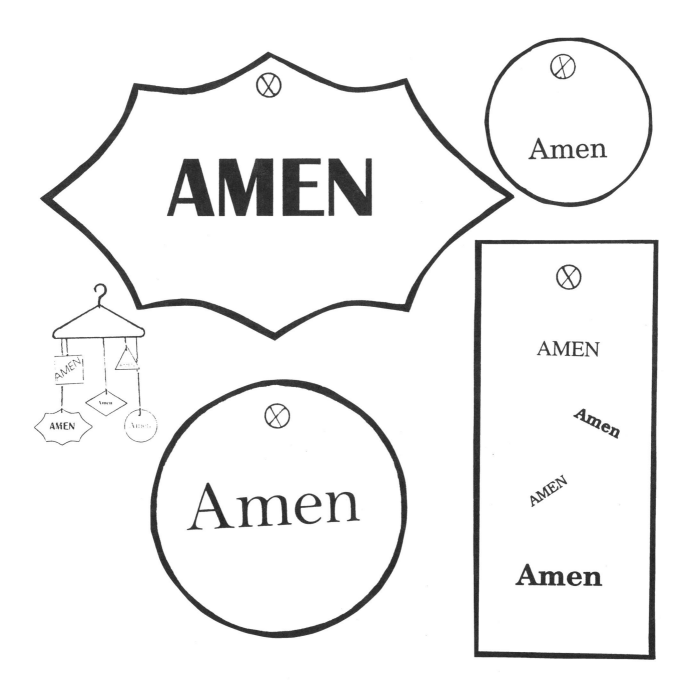

Directions:
1. Color or paint all or some of the Amen patterns.
2. Cut out the Amen patterns. Print a new "Amen" on the back of each pattern.
3. Make more Amen patterns of your own on colored paper shapes.
4. Punch a hole as indicated on each Amen pattern.
5. Use thread or string to hang the Amen patterns from a coat hanger or a loop of yarn.

The Lord's Prayer

Often, we hold hands to say this prayer. By holding hands we show that we are one.
Jesus taught us to pray this prayer.

Directions:

1. Cut page in half on bold centerline.
2. Fold the right piece on the dotted lines accordion style.
3. Hold the folded piece closed with a paper clip. Then cut out the figure on the bold lines.
4. Open and unfold paper dolls.
5. Trim the shirt and hair for the second and fourth figures to make a girl-boy pattern.
6. Decorate.
7. Glue the hand of the first "paper doll" to the boy's hand at "X."
8. Practice saying The Lord's Prayer as you hold the people folded out.
9. Fold and paper clip the dolls for storage.

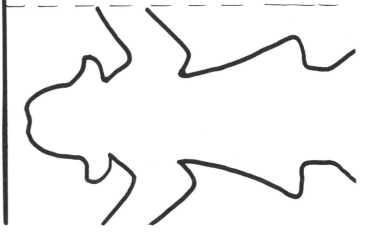

The Lord's Prayer

Our Father, who art in heaven,
hallowed be thy name; thy kingdom
come; thy will be done on earth as it
is in heaven. Give us this day our
daily bread; and forgive us our
trespasses as we forgive those
who trespass against us;
and lead us not into temptation,
but deliver us from
evil.
For the kingdom, the power and the
glory are yours, now and forever.

Sign of Peace

Directions:
1. Color the hands different shades of skin color (e.g., red, brown, peach, black, yellow). Or make copies of the hands on different colors of paper.
2. Cut out the hands.
3. Glue the hands on page 97, two at a time, to appear as if they are shaking hands in the Sign of Peace. (You will have to make separate copies of page 95).

Optional: Make copies of and cut out a second set of hands. Make a "circle of love" wreath out of the hands and glue to page 98. Add a pair of hands by tracing your own.

Priest: Lord Jesus Christ, you said to your apostles: I leave you peace, my peace I give you. Look not on our sins, but on the faith of your Church, and grant us the peace and unity of your kingdom where you live for ever and ever.

We say: **Amen**.

Priest: The peace of the Lord be with you always.

We say: **And also with you**.

Priest or Deacon: Let us offer each other the sign of peace.

Hands of Peace

We shake hands, hug, and offer Christ's peace to all of the people around us at Mass. We show that we are one family in Christ.

"Peace be with you. . ."

Glue the "shaking" hands to this side of the page.

- Have children trace and cut out their own hands and make a huge mural of "Hands of Peace" on brown packaging paper.
- Instruct children on the polite way to shake hands and elicit proper responses.
  Glue the hands in a "circle of love" to this side of the page.

Lamb of God

We are reminded that Jesus died for us and is called the Lamb of God.

Lamb of God, you take away the sins of the world, have mercy on us.
Lamb of God, you take away the sins of the world, have mercy on us.
Lamb of God, you take away the sins of the world, grant us peace.

Directions:
1. Color, paint, or glue glitter to decorate the background.
2. Glue cotton balls on the body of the lamb to add texture.
3. Practice the response, "Lamb of God. . . ."

- Roll up this paper. Secure with a sticker or tie with a ribbon.
- Mount decorated pictures on colored paper.

Communion

Eucharistic Minister

Priest

We sing a song while people are going to communion.

The priest or eucharistic minister holds up the host to each person receiving communion and says, "The body of Christ." The person receiving communion answers "Amen."

Directions:
1. Color and cut both the priest and the eucharistic minister cutouts.
2. Add these cutouts to the Mass scene from Lesson 3, Preparing for Mass.

Make a cutout of you and your family to add to the Lesson 3, Preparing for Mass scene.

5

Concluding Rite

Lesson 27: Final Blessing

Lesson 28: Dismissal

Lesson 27:
Final Blessing

Background

At the conclusion of Mass, the priest offers a final blessing. He calls upon the Trinity. As we are blessed in the name of the Father, and of the Son, and of the Holy Spirit, we are also charged with the duty and pleasure of sharing God's love with others. We are reminded of our uniqueness as we make the Sign of the Cross.

Say to the Students:

As we stand for the final time, the priest lifts his arms up high. We are given a special blessing. We are blessed at the same time because we are one family of God. We listen and bless ourselves, "In the name of the Father, and of the Son, and of the Holy Spirit." Again, we are sharing in a large blanket of love from God. We are accepting the priest's blessing. We are happy to know that we are loved so much. We are reminded of the love and fellowship of Jesus Christ in our daily lives.

Craft/Activity Directions for Final Blessing (pages 107-108)

1. Color the priest.
2. Cut out the priest page on the bold line.
3. Fold the arm at the dotted line.
4. Practice moving the arm to make the Sign of the Cross.
5. Practice saying, "In the name of the Father, and of the Son, and of the Holy Spirit. Amen."

Review Questions

- Who leads the final blessing?
- What do you do and say as you are blessed?
- What does the final blessing remind us to do?

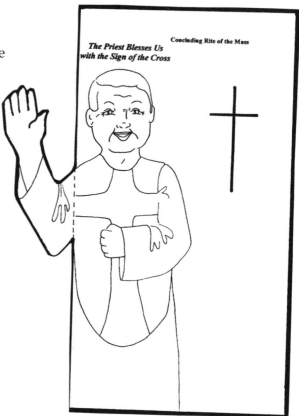

Concluding Rite of the Mass

The Priest Blesses Us with the Sign of the Cross

Lesson 28:
Dismissal

Background

Although this singular service of the Mass is over, we are called to take the love of God out into our daily lives and apply it to our relationships with others. We are reminded to, "Go in peace, to love and serve the Lord." We are to be shining symbols of God's love.

Say to the Students:

At the end of Mass, the priest reminds us to "Go in peace to love and serve the Lord." (Or, "The Mass is ended. Go in peace.") We answer, "Thanks be to God."

As we leave church, we should plan to make the world a better place, to spread the love that we just received during the Mass with all the people we meet. As we deal with others we should be reminded of God's love for us. Does someone treat you unfairly? How would Jesus want you to react? Does someone hurt your feelings? People tried to hurt Jesus, but he told them that love was stronger. We can make a difference. We can spread joy, happiness, and peace.

A heart is a symbol of love. Let's think of ways we can show love. We can make hearts to give to family and friends that we love. We can give these hearts to someone who needs to learn how to love. God's love is a great gift that we all can share.

Craft/Activity Directions for Dismissal Hearts
(pages 109-109)

1. Color the hearts or copy them onto colored paper.
2. Cut out the hearts.
3. Share the hearts and the message they contain with others.

Note: Give each child an envelope or strawberry basket to store their hearts.

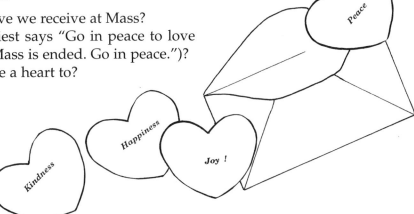

Review Questions

- What should we do with the love we receive at Mass?
- What do you say when the priest says "Go in peace to love and serve the Lord" (or, "The Mass is ended. Go in peace.")?
- Who is someone you might give a heart to?

Children Discover the Mass

The Priest Blesses Us with the Sign of the Cross

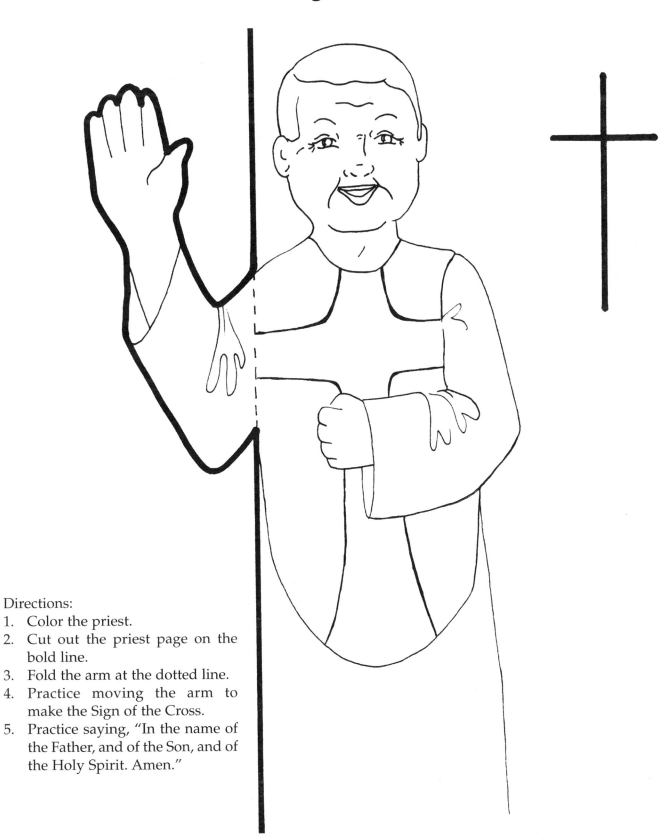

Directions:

1. Color the priest.
2. Cut out the priest page on the bold line.
3. Fold the arm at the dotted line.
4. Practice moving the arm to make the Sign of the Cross.
5. Practice saying, "In the name of the Father, and of the Son, and of the Holy Spirit. Amen."

In the name of the Father,
and of the Son,
and of the Holy Spirit,
   Amen.

Go in peace
to love and serve
the Lord.

Dismissal Heart Cards

As we leave church, we should be going out to make the world a better place, to spread the love that we just received during the Mass with all of the people we meet.

Directions:
1. Color the hearts or copy them onto colored paper.
2. Cut out the hearts.
3. Share the hearts and the message they contain with others.

- Look at the word on the front of the heart. Say it. Copy the word on the back of the heart.
- Decorate an envelope to hold the hearts. Put your name on the envelope.

Appendix

Other activities to help children learn about the Mass:

- Encourage students to draw and tell about their Mass participation.

- Take the students to the empty church and show them the lectern, the altar, etc.

- Have the children make paper place mats showing their family attending Mass. Then share a snack on the place mats. Discuss the Last Supper.

- Ask a priest to come into the classroom with some of the vestments and vessels used during Mass and allow the children to see and touch them.

- Keep several missals on hand for the children to peruse and review.

- Remind the children to look for each part of the Mass when they go to church with their families, and to take some of the activity pages to Mass to use during that part of the Mass. (e.g., Opening Procession, Penitential Rite)

- Make a set of the priest, acolytes, and helpers from Lesson 3, Preparing for Mass, but without the stands. Glue felt on to the backs and allow children to manipulate the pieces using a felt board. Encourage the children to talk about the Mass as they manipulate the figures.

- Make a set of the Lesson 3, Preparing for Mass people and laminate them for use in a "puppet show." Provide a box to use as the church.

- Remind the students that our active participation in Mass is important. Singing brings us closer to God. Practice singing some of the songs used most often at your church with your students.

- While students are working on the craft activities, play some of the more popular songs used at your church.

- Encourage your church nursery to have Mass related crafts available and to play music from the Mass.

- Have the students draw pictures to show how they "go in peace to love and serve the Lord."

- Encourage the children to take "My Mass Book" to church and follow along with the liturgy.

MY MASS BOOK

This book belongs

to _____

We go out into the community.

Dismissal

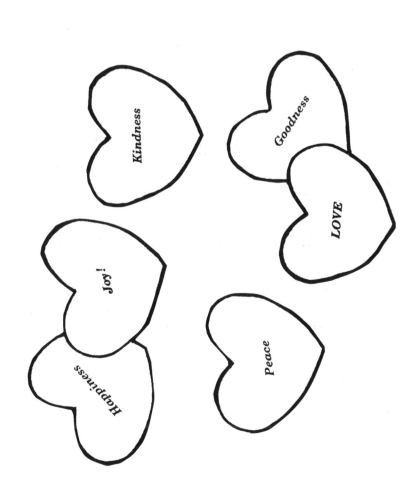

A. Go in the peace of Christ.

or

B. The Mass is ended, go in peace.

or

C. Go in peace to love and serve the Lord.

We say: **Thanks be to God.**

We sing our closing song and go out to share God's love.

We begin. We sing the entrance song.

The Procession

We make the Sign of the Cross.
In the name of the Father, and of the Son, and of the Holy Spirit. +
We say: **Amen.**

We receive God's blessing.

The Blessing

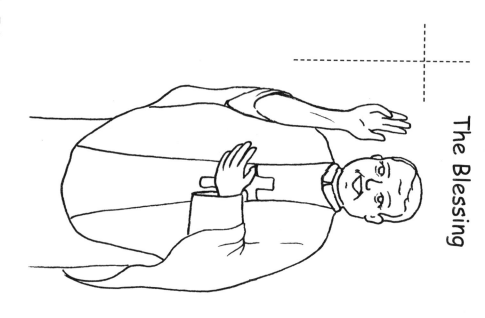

The Priest says: May almighty God bless you, the Father, and the Son, and the Holy Spirit. +
We say: **Amen.**

The Greeting

The Priest says: The grace of our Lord Jesus Christ and the love of God and the fellowship of the Holy Spirit be with you all.

We say: **And also with you.**

OR

The Priest says: The grace and peace of God our Father and the Lord Jesus Christ be with you.

We say: **Blessed be God, the Father of our Lord Jesus Christ.**

OR

And also with you.

OR

The Priest says: The Lord be with you.

We say:

Write **And also with you** on the line.

Prayer After Communion

The Priest says: Let us pray . . . through Christ our Lord.
We say: **Amen.**

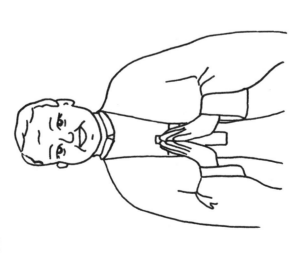

Concluding Rite

Greeting:

The Priest says: The Lord be with you.
We say:

Write **And also with you** on the line.

The Penitential Rite

I confess to almighty God
and to you, my brothers and sisters,
that I have sinned through my own fault
in my thoughts and in my words,
in what I have done,
and in what I have failed to do;
and I ask blessed Mary, ever virgin,
all the angels and saints,
and you, my brothers and sisters,
to pray for me to the Lord our God.

The Priest says: May almighty God have mercy on us, forgive us our sins,
and bring us to everlasting life.
We say: **Amen.**

We receive communion.

A communion song may be sung while communion is given.

Communion

The Priest or Eucharistic Minister says: The body of Christ.
We say: **Amen.**
After communion we return to our seats and pray quietly to Jesus.

We ask Jesus for mercy.

The Kýrie

The Priest says: Lord, have mercy.
We say: **Lord, have mercy.**

The Priest says: Christ, have mercy.
We say: **Christ, have mercy.**

The Priest says: Lord, have mercy.
We say: **Lord, have mercy.**

Sometimes we sing or say this prayer in Greek:

Kýrie, eléison.

Christe, eléison.

Kýrie, eléison.

The Priest receives communion.

Breaking of the Bread

We say: **Lamb of God, you take away the sins of the world: have mercy on us.
Lamb of God, you take away the sins of the world: have mercy on us.
Lamb of God, you take away the sins of the world: grant us peace.**

The Priest says: This is the Lamb of God who takes away the sins of the world.
Happy are those who are called to his supper.

We say with the Priest:
**Lord, I am not worthy to receive you,
but only say the word and I shall be healed.**

We praise God!

The Gloria

Together we say:

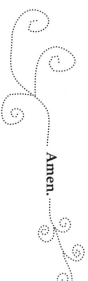

Glory to God in the highest,
and peace to his people on earth.
Lord God, heavenly King,
almighty God and Father,
we worship you, we give you thanks,
we praise you for your glory.
Lord Jesus Christ, only son of the Father,
Lord God, Lamb of God,
you take away the sin of the world:
    have mercy on us;
you are seated at the right hand of the Father:
    receive our prayer.
For you alone are the Holy One,
you alone are the Lord,
you alone are the Most High,
Jesus Christ,
with the Holy Spirit,
in the glory of God the Father.

Amen.

We offer a sign of peace to one another.

The Sign of Peace

The Priest says: Lord Jesus Christ . . . for ever and ever.
We say: **Amen.**

The Priest says: The peace of the Lord be with you always.
We say: **And also with you.**

The Priest says: Let us offer each other a sign of peace.

We pray to God for our needs.

The Opening Prayer

The Priest says: Let us pray.

The Priest says an opening prayer.

Together we say: **Amen.**

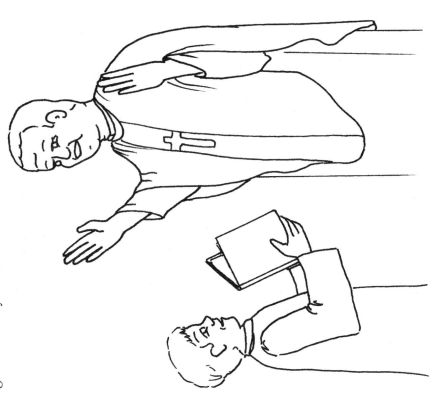

We speak to God using the words Jesus taught us.

The Lord's Prayer

The Priest says: Let us pray with confidence to the Father in the words our Savior gave us:

Together we say:
**Our Father, who art in heaven,
hallowed be thy name;
thy kingdom come;
thy will be done on earth as it is in heaven.
Give us this day our daily bread;
and forgive us our trespasses
as we forgive those who trespass against us;
and lead us not into temptation,
but deliver us from evil.**

The Priest says:
Deliver us, Lord, from every evil,
and grant us peace in our day.
In your mercy keep us free from sin
and protect us from all anxiety
as we wait in joyful hope
for the coming of our Savior, Jesus Christ.

We say:
For the kingdom, the power, and the glory are yours, now and forever.

The Liturgy of the Word:
The First Reading

God speaks to us through our family of faith.

We listen to the word of God.

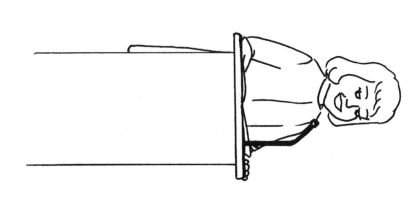

The Lector says: The Word of the Lord.
We say: **Thanks be to God.**

We agree with all that has taken place.

The Great Amen

The Priest says:

Through him,
with him,
in him,

In the unity of the Holy Spirit,
all glory and honor is yours,
almighty Father,
for ever and ever.

We sing or say:

Amen!

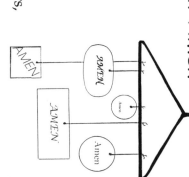

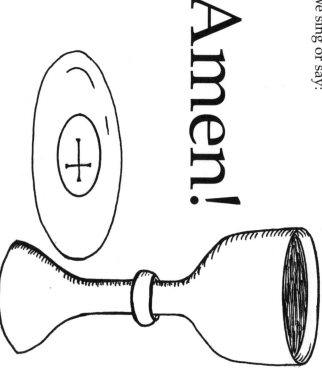

We respond to God's word in a Psalm.

Responsorial Psalm

We repeat a psalm
or sing a psalm of response.

The Second Reading

God speaks to us through the words of the first Christians.

The Lector says: The Word of the Lord.

We say: **Thanks be to God.**

We proclaim our faith.

Memorial Acclamation

The Priest says: Let us proclaim the mystery of faith:

We say:
**Christ has died,
Christ is risen,
Christ will come again.**

OR

**Dying you destroyed our death,
rising you restored our life.
Lord Jesus, come in glory.**

OR

**When we eat this bread and drink this cup,
we proclaim your death, Lord Jesus,
until you come in glory.**

OR

**Lord, by your cross and resurrection
you have set us free.
You are the Savior of the world.**

God speaks to us through the words and actions of Jesus.
We stand and listen.

The Gospel

The Priest says: The Lord be with you.
We say: **And also with you.**

The Priest or Deacon says: A reading from the holy gospel according to _____.

We say: **Glory to you, Lord.**

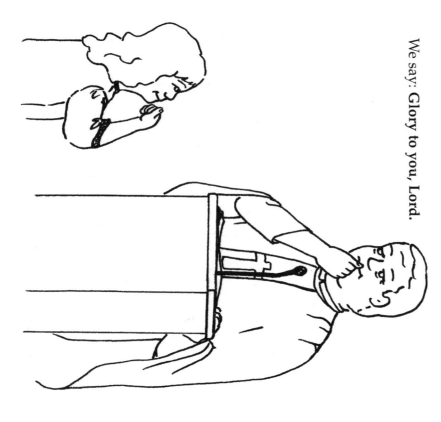

Consecration of the Wine

The blessed wine becomes the Blood of Jesus as the Priest says the same words Jesus said at the Last Supper.

The Priest says:
Take this, all of you, and drink from it:
this is the cup of my blood,
the blood of the new and everlasting covenant.

It will be shed for you and for all
So that sins may be forgiven.

Do this in memory of me.

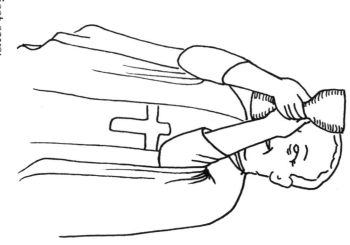

The Priest or Deacon speaks to us.

The Homily

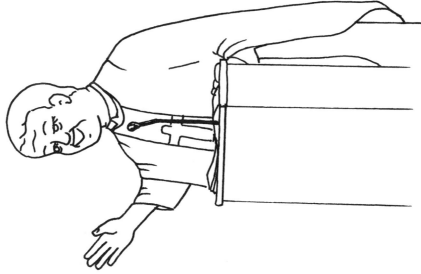

The blessed bread becomes the body of Christ.
The Priest holds up the blessed host. Then, the host is placed on the paten. The Priest genuflects.

Consecration of the Bread

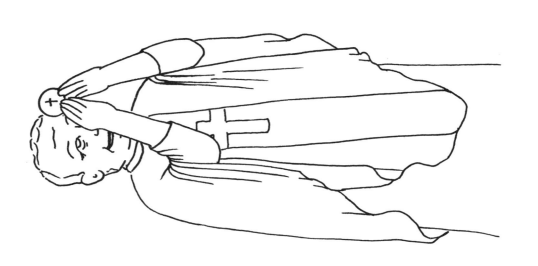

The Nicene Creed

We believe in one God,
  The Father, the Almighty,
  maker of heaven and earth,
  of all that is seen and unseen.

We believe in one Lord, Jesus Christ,
  the only Son of God,
  eternally begotten of the Father,
  God from God, Light from Light,
  true God from true God,
  begotten, not made, one in Being with the Father.
  Through him all things were made.
  For us men and for our salvation
    he came down from heaven:
by the power of the Holy Spirit
  he was born of the Virgin Mary, and became man.
For our sake he was crucified under Pontius Pilate;
  he suffered, died, and was buried.
  On the third day he rose again
    in fulfillment of the Scriptures;
  he ascended into heaven
    and is seated at the right hand of the Father.
He will come again in glory to judge the living and the dead,
  and his kingdom will have no end.
We believe in the Holy Spirit, the Lord, the giver of life,
  who proceeds from the Father and the Son.
  With the Father and the Son he is worshiped and glorified.
He has spoken through the Prophets.
We believe in one holy catholic and apostolic Church.
We acknowledge one baptism for the forgiveness of sins.
We look for the resurrection of the dead,
  and the life of the world to come.

Amen.

Jesus blessed bread and wine and gave it to his disciples.

The Last Supper

The Priest repeats the words of Jesus:
  Take this, all of you, and eat it: this is my body which will be
given up for you.

Profession of Faith

The Apostles' Creed

I believe in God, the Father almighty,
　　creator of heaven and earth.
I believe in Jesus Christ, his only Son, our Lord.
　　He was conceived by the power of the Holy Spirit
　　　and born of the Virgin Mary.
He suffered under Pontius Pilate,
　　was crucified, died, and was buried.
He descended to the dead.
On the third day he rose again.
He ascended into heaven,
　　and is seated at the right hand of the Father.
He will come again to judge the living and the dead.
I believe in the Holy Spirit,
　　the holy catholic Church
　　the communion of saints, the forgiveness of sins,
　　the resurrection of the body,
　　and the life everlasting. Amen.

General Intercessions

We pray for the needs of our Church and the world.

We say: **Lord, hear our prayer.** (Or other response.)

The Priest says a prayer.

We say: **Amen.**

Our Gifts

The Priest calls on the Holy Spirit.

Lord, we pray that the Holy Spirit
may come upon these gifts
and make them holy.

May they become for us
the body and blood
of our Lord Jesus Christ.

The Liturgy of the Eucharist:

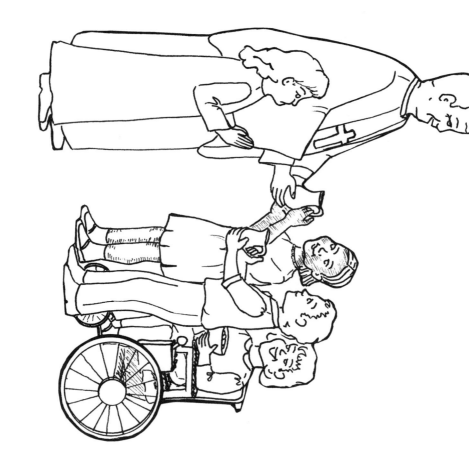

Preparation of the Altar
We bring our gifts to the altar.

Holy, Holy, Holy

We say:
Holy, Holy, Holy Lord,
    God of power and might.
Heaven and earth are full of your glory.
    Hosanna in the highest.
Blessed is he who comes in the name of the Lord.
    Hosanna in the highest.

Preparation of the Bread

The Priest says:
Blessed are you, Lord, God of all creation.
Through your goodness we have this bread to offer,
Which earth has given and human hands have made.
It will become for us the bread of life.

We say: **Blessed be God for ever.**

Preparation of the Wine

The Priest says:
Blessed are you, Lord, God of all creation.
Through your goodness we have
this wine to offer,
Fruit of the vine and work
of human hands.
It will become our spiritual drink.

We say: **Blessed be God for ever.**

The Eucharistic Prayer

The Priest says: The Lord be with you.
We say: **And also with you.**

The Priest says: Lift up your hearts.
We say: **We lift them up to the Lord.**

The Priest says: Let us give thanks to the Lord our God.
We say: **It is right to give him thanks and praise.**

The Preface

The Priest prays and we listen. Then we joyfully sing
Holy, Holy, Holy together.

We ask God to accept our gifts.

Invitation to Prayer

The Priest says: Pray, brothers and sisters, that our sacrifice may be acceptable to God, the almighty Father.

We say: **May the Lord accept the sacrifice
at your hands
for the praise and glory of his name,
for our good, and the good of all his Church.**

The Priest prays over the gifts.
We say: **Amen.**

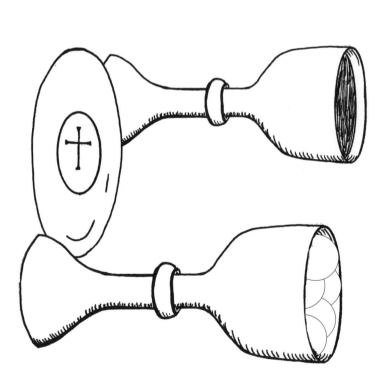